Sikhi Quest

Discover The Guru's Path

DR PARMINDER SINGH SAHOTA

Contents

The Author

drp.s.sahota@gmail.com

This book is a reflection of the profound influence of my Guru, without whom its creation would not have been possible. No amount of worldly knowledge, degrees, or experiences can match the depth of wisdom bestowed by the Guru's grace.

To love without conditions, to embrace each moment without judgment, is to open oneself to the true essence of life. It goes beyond surrender or acceptance; it is simply being present in the purest form.

There is no need to search for answers outside ourselves; we are born complete; with all we need within us. My Guru teaches us to refrain from disrupting the natural flow of life and to release ourselves from reactive actions.

Through the teachings of my Guru, life unfolds with new insights, and I continue to learn and grow. With the Guru's guidance, I embrace my roles as a husband, father, uncle, friend, and grandfather, allowing love and wisdom to shape my journey. GurKirpa!

Introduction to the Book (Parents)

The phrase "to study the old is to understand the new" encapsulates the idea that knowledge of historical or traditional contexts is essential for comprehending and navigating contemporary situations or developments.

Studying the old allows us to contextualize the new within a broader framework of human experience and knowledge. It equips us with the perspective and wisdom necessary to navigate the complexities of the present and shape a more informed and enlightened future.

Sikhi was established at a time when there was spiritual, political, and cultural upheaval in India. It began with the teachings of Guru Nanak Dev Ji. Who was deeply influenced by the religious and social turmoil of his time, which included the dominance of the caste system, religious orthodoxy, rituals, and the inequalities prevalent in society even today.

Humanity had become distorted by the society by doing things for the wrong reasons. Sikhi provided a path back to a revisit to the original messages of love, compassion, forgiveness, and trust.

Guru Nanak Ji was on a mission to move society away from suffering, division, and controversy to one of universal cohesiveness. He wanted to establish a society that would flourish and prosper. From being self-serving to one that served others. The Sikh Gurus and indeed the eternal Siri Guru Granth Sahib Ji carries this mission forward today and will do so forever.

This book is based on both first-hand experiences and personal conversations with Sangat. These experiences guided my personal journey that began with a diagnosis of critical heart failure following a heart attack in 1996 at the age of thirty-nine. and helped crystallise my subsequent enquiry about the purpose and meaning of my life.

So began my journey into Sikhi anew. Seeing with my heart as well as my emotions. Facing my perceptions and daily living with challenging honesty. Looking at my actions as well as intention. Am I really what I appear to myself and others. Sikhs continually check and evaluate themselves.

To not do this is to drift away into what we think we see and do rather than what is actual. I went back to my teacher to avoid this drift and stay focussed upon the essence of Sikhi. I have used the teacher to share my understanding with you. Sri Guru Granth Sahib Ji Maharaj. A collection and distillation of the essence of Sikhi.

When my mind opened to my own shortcomings and the desire to be better informed, more authentic, and truer to what I believed, it also opened me to conversations with sangat mostly at my local Gurdwara. As well as not only deepening my understanding of Gurbani it also brought to my attention the hunger of both parents and children to develop a foundational understanding of Sikhi. This book is for them. For parents and children.

The book is organized into four sections. The initial segment covers fundamental aspects of spirituality, Sikh

Dharma, the Sikh Gurus, Gurmukhi, Siri Guru Granth Sahib Ji, Dhasam and Sarbloh, Granths, Miri Piri, Khalsa, Amrit Sanchar, and related topics.

It also delves into essential aspects such as the Gurdwara, the Takhts, Nishan Sahib, Khanda, a Giani, Sangat, Kirtan, Katha, and Matha Tekh. This segment is designated as FI (Foundational Information).

The second section of the book coves key practices in Sikhi. These include Nitnem, Ardhas, Jaap, Simran, Seva, Vand Chako, Naam Japo, Kirat Kamai and Karah Parshad. These practices help develop the personal discipline and inward-looking and outward-seeking focus on the divine. This section is marked KP (Key Practices).

The third section covers key teachings of Sikhi based on the sense I have tried to make of them. Gurbani is a vast ocean, and my knowledge is limited to a few drops of the oceans spray that, with Guru's Kirpa, have touched me. The teachings include explanations of key teachings such as Ek Onkar, Mool, Hukam, Maya, Karma, Gurprashad, Waheguru, Haumai, Mool Mantar, Naam, Anand, Anand Karaj and many more. This section is marked KT (Key Teachings)

The concluding section of the book presents crucial messages, once more graciously bestowed by the Guru's Kirpa, as conveyed by the author. It encompasses Gurmat, practical advice for parents, and a concluding message inspired by the timeless Siri Guru Granth Sahib Ji. These messages distil elements of teachings that we can take beyond our minds and into our daily lives. This section is designated as KM (Key Messages).

The sections do not stand in isolation from each other. You have the flexibility to explore any topic that captures your interest, in any sequence you prefer.

My humble Ardhas (prayer) is that this book helps develop a good understanding of Sikhi and, with Guru's Kirpa, spark an interest in readers to explore it further to contribute to your understanding about how we can live a life guided by the wisdom of our Gurus.

With faith and trust in the Guru, this journey will be one filled with wonder and awe. You will discover that you are much more that this body of flesh and bones. You are the Mool – the very thing that that you seek and indeed the very thing that is seeking you.

'I searched for God and found only myself. I searched for myself and found only God.' - Rumi

Wahe Guru Ji ka Khalsa Waheguru Ji Ki Fateh

Introduction to the Book (Children)

Once upon a time, there was a wise saying that goes like this: "To study the old is to understand the new." What does that mean? Well, imagine you have a big puzzle. The old pieces of the puzzle are like the history of the puzzle, and the new pieces are what is happening right now. If you do not know about the old pieces, it is like trying to finish the puzzle without seeing the picture on the box. Studying the old helps us make sense of the new!

Long ago, there was an incredibly special time in India. People were confused about what was right and wrong, and things were very mixed up. That is when a wise person named Guru Nanak Dev Ji came along. He saw that people were treating each other unfairly and wanted to help them find their way back to kindness and love.

Guru Nanak Ji taught everyone about love, forgiveness, and trust. He wanted to make the world a better place where everyone could live happily together. His teachings were so important that they are still followed today by people called Sikhs.

This book is written by someone who went on a journey to learn more about Guru Nanak Ji and the Sikh way of life. It is divided into various parts to help you understand things step by step. You can learn about spirituality, important Sikh teachings, and practices like prayer and helping others.

In this special book about Sikhi, there are some important messages that the author wants to share with you. These messages are like guiding lights that can help you understand life better and become a better person.

One of the key messages is about Gurmat. Gurmat means the wisdom or teachings of the Guru. It is all about learning from Guru Nanak Ji and the other Sikh Gurus. Their teachings are like precious gems that can show us how to live in a good and kind way.

The book also gives practical tips for parents. Parents play a key role in instructing their children about Sikhi and helping them grow into good people. So, these tips are like helpful hints for moms and dads to make learning about Sikhi fun and interesting for their kids.

And finally, there is a closing message inspired by the eternal Siri Guru Granth Sahib Ji. This message is like a special note from the heart of Sikhi itself. It is filled with love, wisdom, and encouragement to keep learning and growing on your journey of understanding Sikhi.

So, as you read through this book, pay close attention to these key messages. They are like treasures waiting to be discovered, and they can help you become the best version of yourself.

Waheguru Ji Ka Khalsa Waheguru Ji Ki Fateh

ਰੂਹਾਨੀਅਤ

Spirituality (FI)

Let us go on a super cool adventure into the world of spirituality.

Imagine spirituality like putting on magical glasses. But instead of changing what you see, they make you see the world in a distinct way. Just like having a secret power to understand how amazing everything is around us.

Do you know those times when you see something awesome, like a rainbow or a cute puppy, and you feel all warm inside? That is what spirituality is all about - feeling really connected to everything in the world, even stuff we can't see.

Think of yourself as the hero in a fantastic storybook, discovering ancient tales and traditions that are like hidden treasures. These stories help us understand why things happen and how we fit into the big picture.

But spirituality is not just about stories; It is about experiencing wonder and magic. Like looking at the stars at night or walking through a beautiful forest and feeling amazed by how incredible the world is.

And guess what? Everyone experiences spirituality in their own distinct way. Just like how you have a favourite flavour of ice cream, people find spirituality in different things. Some people feel it when they pray or meditate, while others feel it when they are kind to others or spend time with family and friends.

And here is something cool: spirituality isn't just for serious stuff. It is in all the fun things we do, like playing with toys or laughing with our buddies.

So, spirituality is an amazing journey where we explore the mysteries of life and find joy in everything around us. Feeling connected to something bigger than ourselves and finding meaning in everything we do.

And the best part? We are all on this journey together, holding hands and having a blast!

ਧਰਮ and ਮਜਬ

Dharma and Religion (FI)

Imagine *dharma* as your special guidebook for living life. It is akin to having a set of rules that help you be the best version of yourself. Just like how you follow the rules when you play a game, *dharma* guides you in making good choices in life.

Now, think of *religion* as a big community or team where people who believe in the same things come together. It is the same as being on a team where everyone supports each other and cheers each other on.

One cool thing about both *dharma* and *religion* is that they are all about being kind and helping others. It is like when you share your toys with your friends or give a hug to someone who is sad. Both *dharma* and *religion* say that spreading love and kindness is super important.

But there is a slight difference between them: *dharma* helps you make decisions in your own life, like how to be a good friend or how to do your chores well.

On the other hand, *religion* is more about following the beliefs and traditions of your community, like going to religious ceremonies or celebrating special holidays with your family.

So, even though *dharma* and *religion* both lead to goodness and happiness, they do it in slightly different ways. It is comparable to having two different recipes for making cookies—they might have some of the same ingredients, but they end up tasting a little different.

Pretty interesting, right?

ਸਿੱਖ ਧਰਮ

A Sikh and Sikh Dharam (FI)

Being a *Sikh* is like being a super awesome student who is always excited to learn and grow spiritually. The word *"Sikh"* comes from Punjabi, which means a "learner" or a "disciple."

It is akin to being a student of wise teachers, called the Sikh Gurus. But being a *Sikh* is not just about listening to what the Gurus say, it is about doing what they teach us, like being kind and helping others, even when things are tough.

I have learned this from my own experiences, facing challenges and growing because of them.

A *Sikh* always wants to learn more and be a better person with a big heart full of love for everyone. A *Sikh* is one who also practices what the Guru teaches. The Gurus teach us to keep growing inside, to be kind to everyone, and to remember that we are all connected like a big family.

Sikhi began about five hundred years ago in Punjab, India. Guru Nanak Dev Ji was the founder and first Guru and was succeeded by other Gurus.

Here are some important things that Sikhs believe in:

We believe in one supreme God, who connects us all.

We respect our spiritual guide, the Guru Granth Sahib.

We value the Sikh community and our sacred texts.

We think everyone should be treated equally, no matter how different they are.

We believe in being kind and helping others.

We believe in working hard and being honest.

We find peace in praying and meditating to get closer to God.

We go to our special places of worship called Gurdwaras to pray and share meals together.

We stand up for what's right and fight against what is wrong.

We do not focus on fancy rituals or superstitions; we believe in keeping things simple and good.

These beliefs are important to Sikhs, and they shape how we live our lives every day.

Being a *Sikh* is not just about saying we're Sikhs; it is about living by these teachings and making the world better for everyone.

Pretty simple huh?

ਸਿੱਖ ਗੁਰੂ

Sikh Gurus (FI)

Picture this: our *Gurus* are like shining beacons of light, illuminating our path through life's mysteries. They are not just ordinary teachers; they're our superheroes, guiding us through the twists and turns of our own epic adventure.

Now, let us decode the magic of the word *Guru* itself. *"Gu"* means darkness, and *"ru"* means light. So, a *Guru* is like a radiant torch, banishing the shadows of confusion and leading us into the bright realm of understanding.

It is as if they flick on a switch in our minds, revealing clarity, joy, and boundless hope.

Think of darkness as those moments of doubt or sadness, and light as the feeling of clarity, happiness, and optimism that fills our hearts. In Sikhi, the *Guru* is not just a distant figure; they are our closest confidants, guiding us with unwavering love and support, especially when the going gets tough.

Even though we cannot see them with our eyes, the wisdom of our *Gurus* lives on in the timeless words of the Siri Guru Granth Sahib Ji, our eternal guide. They are walking right beside us, holding our hands through every twist and turn of life's journey.

Each *Guru* is a shining star in the night sky, guiding us through life's adventures with their wisdom and kindness.

Imagine *Guru Nanak Dev Ji,* the very first Guru, spreading the message of love and equality like colourful petals in the wind. He showed us that no matter who we are or where we come from, we are all part of one big family. He also stared Langar that we all love to have.

Then there's *Guru Angad Dev Ji*, who created a special alphabet so that everyone could read the beautiful words of our Gurus. He made sure that nobody was left behind, opening the doors of knowledge to all.

Guru Amar Das Ji taught us to share and care for one another, just like a family sharing a delicious meal. He showed us that a little kindness goes a long way in making the world a better place.

Guru Ram Das Ji built the Golden Temple, a place where people of all backgrounds can come together and find peace. It is like a warm hug from our Guru, welcoming us home.

And *Guru Arjan Dev Ji*, he put together the Adi Granth, filling it with pearls of wisdom to guide us through life's difficulties. He made sure that we always have a friend to turn to, even in our darkest hours.

Guru Hargobind Ji was strong and brave, like a mighty lion protecting his pride. He taught us to stand tall in the face of challenges, never backing down from what we believe in.

Guru Har Rai Ji loved all of nature's creatures, from the tiniest ant to the mightiest elephant. He showed us that compassion is the greatest gift we can give to the world around us.

And *Guru Har Krishan Ji*, though young, had a heart as big as the sky. He cared for the sick and the suffering, spreading hope and healing wherever he went.

Guru Tegh Bahadur Ji stood up for what was right, even when it was hard. He taught us that sometimes, being brave means standing alone for what we believe in.

And *Guru Gobind Singh Ji*, our warrior Guru, who created the Khalsa, a family of brave souls ready to protect and serve others. He showed us that true strength comes from within, fuelled by love and courage.

And finally, our eternal *Guru Granth Sahib ji* which is a very special treasure chest filled with wisdom and love. Inside, there are lots of teachings and stories that help us understand how to be kind, brave, and good people.

As you walk along the path of life, remember the lessons of our *Gurus*. Be kind, be brave, and most importantly, be true to yourself.

For in their teachings, you will find the light to guide you through even the darkest of nights.

ਗੁਰਮੁਖੀ

ੳ	ਅ	ੲ	ਸ	ਹ
ਕ	ਖ	ਗ	ਘ	ਙ
ਚ	ਛ	ਜ	ਝ	ਞ
ਟ	ਠ	ਡ	ਢ	ਣ
ਤ	ਥ	ਦ	ਧ	ਨ
ਪ	ਫ	ਬ	ਭ	ਮ
ਯ	ਰ	ਲ	ਵ	ੜ
ਸ਼	ਖ਼	ਗ਼	ਜ਼	ਟ

Gurmukhi (FI)

Gurmukhi is a treasure trove of wisdom and wonder awaiting our eager exploration!

Let us journey back in time to meet two remarkable Gurus who gifted us something truly extraordinary: Guru Angad Dev Ji and Guru Arjan Dev Ji.

Guru Angad Dev Ji, our second Guru saw that many people found it hard to understand the teachings of Sikhi because the scripts were too tricky. So, with boundless love and wisdom, he created something amazing called *Gurmukhi.*

It is like a magic key that unlocks the treasure chest of Sikh wisdom for everyone to enjoy!

It is no surprise that *Gurmukhi* means "words from the mouth of the Guru"!

And then, along came Guru Arjan Dev Ji, a beacon of light in our history. He took Guru Angad Dev Ji's gift of *Gurmukhi* and did something truly miraculous. He used it to compile the Adi Granth that later became the Siri Guru Granth Sahib Ji, our eternal guide. Can you imagine?

The Gurus transformed words into jewels, filling our hearts with joy and wisdom with every turn of the page.

Gurmukhi is not just a set of letters; It is a magical gateway to a world filled with stories of bravery, compassion, and love. It is our very own map guiding us through the adventures of Sikhi with grace and beauty.

Imagine *Gurmukhi* as a colourful tapestry woven with threads of love and wisdom by our wise Gurus. Each letter holds a secret, waiting to be unlocked, revealing the timeless truths of our faith.

Learning *Gurmukhi* is more than just a task; It is an exciting quest to uncover the hidden gems left behind by our incredible Gurus. With each word we learn, we draw closer to the heart of Sikhi, connecting with our heritage and our identity as proud Sikhs.

But *Gurmukhi* is not just about reading; It is about speaking from the soul. When we recite prayers and hymns in *Gurmukhi*, we are not just uttering words; we're communicating directly with Waheguru, our beloved creator.

And here is the most amazing part: *Gurmukhi* is a bridge that connects us to our past and to Sikhs all around the world. It is a language of unity, bringing us together as one big family, bound by our shared faith and values.

As you embark on your journey of learning *Gurmukhi*, remember this: you are not just mastering a language; you're embracing a legacy. You are stepping into the footsteps of our Gurus, carrying their light forward into the world.

With each letter you learn, with each word you speak, you are weaving a beautiful tapestry of love, faith, and courage. So, keep shining bright, keep learning, and keep spreading the timeless wisdom of Gurmukhi wherever you go.

whenever you read *Gurmukhi,* remember the incredible journey of Guru Angad Dev Ji and Guru Arjan Dev Ji. They did not just give us letters; they gave us a treasure beyond compare. And now, it is up to us to cherish it, learn from it, and share its light with the world.

ਜੋਰੇ ਦੀ ਕਹਾਣੀ

Jora's Short Story (FI)

In a peaceful village nestled amidst rolling hills and lush greenery, there lived a young Sikh boy named Jora. Jora was filled with an insatiable curiosity about the world around him and a deep longing to understand the teachings of Sikhi.

One bright morning, as the golden sun rose above the horizon, Jora sat beneath the shade of a towering banyan tree, gazing at the tranquil beauty of nature. As he watched the leaves dance in the gentle breeze, he felt a stirring within his soul, a calling to embark on a journey of spiritual discovery.

With a determined gleam in his eye, Jora decided that today would be the day he began his quest to learn more about Sikhi. Gathering his courage, he made his way to the village gurdwara, the sacred place where the Siri Guru Granth Sahib, the holy scripture of the Sikhs, resided.

As Jora stepped inside the gurdwara, he was enveloped in a sense of peace and serenity. The air was filled with the melodious strains of kirtan, the devotional singing of hymns from the Guru Granth Sahib. Mesmerized by the enchanting music, Jora felt a deep sense of connection to something greater than himself.

Approaching the Guru Granth Sahib with reverence, Jora bowed his head in prayer, his heart overflowing with devotion. With trembling hands, he traced the words of the sacred scripture in Gurmukhi, the divine script of the

Sikhs, eager to soak in the wisdom contained within its pages.

As Jora delved into the teachings of Sikhi, he discovered a profound sense of purpose and meaning in life. He learned about the importance of living a life of honesty and integrity, guided by the principles of spirituality and dharma.

Day by day, Jora's understanding of Sikhi deepened, and his love for Waheguru, the divine creator, grew stronger. He found solace in the timeless wisdom of the Guru Granth Sahib and took solace in its teachings during times of joy and sorrow.

With each passing moment, Jora felt himself becoming more connected to his Sikh heritage and more aligned with the path of honesty laid out by the Gurus. And as he continued his journey into Sikhi, he knew that he was walking in the footsteps of the great spiritual warriors who had come before him.

Filled with gratitude for the opportunity to explore the depths of his faith, Jora vowed to dedicate his life to living according to the teachings of Sikhi and spreading the message of love, compassion, and unity to all who crossed his path.

And so, dear friends, Jora's journey into Sikhi had only just begun, but already his heart was filled with a profound sense of peace and purpose. For he knew that as long as he remained dedicated in his devotion to Waheguru and committed to walking the path of goodness, he would continue to find fulfilment and joy in every step of the way.

ਗੁਰੂ ਗ੍ਰੰਥ ਸਾਹਿਬ

ਡਿਠੇ ਸਭੇ ਥਾਵ ਨਹੀ ਤੁਧੁ ਜੇਹਿਆ

The Siri Guru Granth Sahib Ji (SGGS) (FI)

Once upon a time, our wise Gurus wrote down their teachings in a special manuscript called the *Adi Granth*. It was like a treasure chest filled with stories, songs, and wisdom to guide us on our journey through life.

But as time passed, something magical happened. Our tenth Guru, Guru Gobind Singh Ji, did something amazing. He added more wise words and teachings from our Gurus and other holy people, making the *Adi Granth* even more special.

And thus, the Adi Granth became the *Siri Guru Granth Sahib Ji*! Our forever Guru, always there to show us the right way to go.

So, picture the *Siri Guru Granth Sahib Ji (SGGS)* as a gigantic treasure chest overflowing with positivity and blessings from our revered Gurus and saints. As a source of inspiration, helping us express ourselves, learn new things, and reminding us that every person deserves love and respect, no matter who they are.

So, whenever we read from the SGGS, we are connecting with our Gurus, feeling their love, and learning how to be kind, brave, and strong, just like them. It is a melody of wisdom and love, resonating in our hearts as *Shabad* or *Gurbani*.

It is as if we are receiving messages from a trusted messenger, guiding us on our path with grace and kindness.

As a Sikh, whenever I read from the *SGGS*, I feel wrapped in warmth and guidance. It is like receiving a big, comforting hug filled with love and invaluable advice, empowering me to stand tall and believe in myself.

It is as though our Guru is right beside us, whispering words of encouragement: "You are strong, you are important. Embrace who you are, fearlessly. I am always here with you."

And the cool part is that the *SGGS* is not just for a select few - it is a guiding beacon for all. A living Guru, sharing wisdom from our Gurus and wise souls from across the globe. Though they come from diverse backgrounds, their message remains the same - love and integrity.

The amazing fact is that the *SGGS* is not just another manuscript—it is our Guru in tangible form! That is why each page is called an *"Ang,"* which means a physical part of Guru Ji, signifying its profound significance to us. Every word within is believed to emanate directly from Waheguru, making it sacred and extraordinary.

Just as we honour our Gurus, we treat the *SGGS* with utmost reverence. Through traditions like *Parkash* and *Sukhasan*, we show our respect and devotion. *Parkash* is a grand ceremony where we unveil the *SGGS*, offering prayers and listening to its divine message with deep reverence. *Sukhasan* is when we tenderly put the *SGGS* to rest for the night, ensuring its comfort and safety.

During these traditions, we use a special whisk known as *Chaur Sahib* as a symbol of respect and service. In our Gurdwaras, serving others holds immense significance, and waving the *Chaur Sahib* is one way we express love and respect to the *SGGS* and our community.

So, cherish the *Siri Guru Granth Sahib Ji* like a precious treasure. Let its words be your guiding light as you journey through life's difficulties. And remember, you are never alone because your Guru is always by your side, guiding you with love and wisdom every step of the way. Keep shining bright!

ਦਸਮ ਗ੍ਰੰਥ & ਸਰਬਲੋਹ ਗ੍ਰੰਥ

Dhasam and Sarbloh Granths (Fl)

The *Dasam Granth* and the *Sarbloh Granth* are two remarkable treasures within our Sikh heritage. Picture them as grand chests overflowing with precious gems, waiting to be uncovered by seekers like you!

The *Dasam Granth*, crafted by our Tenth Guru, Guru Gobind Singh Ji, is a testament to courage, love, and morality. Within its pages lie tales that ignite bravery and inspire the soul. It is not just stories; it is a beacon of hope, guiding us through life's trials with unwavering resolve.

From the valorous accounts of battles to heartfelt expressions of devotion, every word in the *Dasam Granth* speaks of resilience and faith. It reminds us of Guru Gobind Singh Ji's unwavering commitment to justice and fairness, urging us to emulate his noble ideals in our own lives.

Similarly, the *Sarbloh Granth* echoes the spirit of our warrior-saint Guru Gobind Singh Ji, urging us to embody strength and valour in all our endeavours. Like a steadfast companion, it reminds us to stand tall in the face of adversity and uphold the values of honesty, humility, and compassion.

Just as the Guru Granth Sahib teaches us to love and revere Waheguru, these writings instil in us the courage to confront life's challenges head-on. They serve as guiding lights, illuminating our path with wisdom and fortitude, reminding us that we are destined for greatness.

Both *Granths* hold immense significance for Sikhs, particularly those who adhere to the martial tradition, like the Nihang Singhs.

So, let the stories within these sacred texts ignite the fire of courage within you. Let them inspire you to be the best version of yourself, to stand up for what is right, and to tread the path of justice with unwavering determination.

Keep exploring, keep learning, and never forget the power that lies within you.

ਮੀਰੀ-ਪੀਰੀ

Miri Peri (FI)

Miri Piri which is about discovering the balance between our spiritual path and our daily experiences. It is as simple as that.

Imagine this: *Miri* means being strong in the world, while *Piri* means having spiritual strength. It is like saying we should be as sturdy as a mountain in what we do and as radiant as the sun in what we believe.

A long time ago, Guru Hargobind Sahib, our sixth Sikh Guru, showed us the magic of *Miri Piri* by carrying two swords. One sword was a symbol of spiritual power, and the other represented worldly strength. Why? Because back then, life was tough for Sikhs, and they needed to stand tall against unfairness.

To keep Sikhs safe, Guru Hargobind Sahib made them strong and built the Akal Takht, a place where Sikh leaders could gather to make important decisions. And guess what? It was right next to Harmandir Sahib, the Golden Temple, our spiritual hub.

Our Gurus taught us something special: we need to be kind and gentle from the inside but brave and resilient on the outside. They wanted us to be like peaceful warriors, ready to protect ourselves and others.

But guess what? This idea is not just for the past. It is super relevant today! It encourages Sikhs to step out into the world and fight for what is right, spreading goodness and fairness wherever they go.

Now, let us talk about another awesome concept: a *Santh Sipahi*, or Saint-Soldier. It means being deeply devoted to Waheguru and being prepared to stand up for justice, even if it means facing tough battles.

This idea shines brightly in the Khalsa, which was founded by our tenth Guru, Guru Gobind Singh Ji. It is about being spiritually awake, bold, and ready to fight against anything unfair or unjust.

Miri Piri and being a Saint-Soldier are like our guiding lights, showing us how to live honourably and protect those in need. It guides us to be kind-hearted warriors, standing up for what is right and fair.

And have you ever noticed something fascinating about the Sikh flag, the Nishan Sahib? It proudly displays two crossed swords, symbolizing *Miri* and *Piri*—being strong in the world and firm in our beliefs. Pretty cool, right?

So, imagine yourself as a brave knight, strong and courageous in the world, but also gentle and kind inside. That is what *Miri Piri* is all about! Just like the superheroes you love, our Sikh Gurus showed us how to be strong and stand up for what is right, while also being filled with love and compassion.

As you journey through life, remember to be as brave as a lion and as peaceful as a dove. Keep *Miri Piri* in your heart, and you will always shine bright like a star!

Go out there and spread goodness wherever you go, because you are a true hero in the making!

ਖ਼ਾਲਸਾ

Khalsa (FI)

Sikhs and Khalsa? Let us try to understand this a little bit more.

Imagine being a Sikh, walking the path set by the ten Sikh Gurus, with the Siri Guru Granth Sahib Ji as your eternal guide. Sikhs are like shining stars, devoted to one God, treating everyone with kindness and equality, and spreading goodness wherever they go.

And a Khalsa? *Khalsa* means "pure," and it is like being part of an elite squad within Sikhi, established by the visionary Guru Gobind Singh in 1699. Khalsa members follow some special rules and have a distinctive appearance.

They proudly wear five sacred symbols: the Punj Kakar, uncut hair, a comb, a bracelet, cotton undergarments, and a kirpan.

To join the *Khalsa*, you undergo a special ceremony called Amrit Sanchar. It is a solemn moment where you drink Amrit, a sacred elixir, to signify your unwavering commitment to the *Khalsa* way of life.

The birth of the *Khalsa* marked a pivotal moment in Sikh history, happening on April 13, 1699, during the joyful festival of Vaisakhi. Guru Gobind Singh believed deeply in the need for the *Khalsa* to stand against injustice and uplift those facing unfair treatment.

But here is the real magic—the *Khalsa* isn't just about spirituality. It is about bravery and standing up for what is right. Guru Gobind Singh envisioned the *Khalsa* as warriors of both spirit and body, embodying the concept of *Miri-Piri*—strength in both the physical and spiritual realms.

The *Khalsa's* mission is clear: to champion fairness and aid those in need. Guru Gobind Singh likened the *Khalsa* to a divine army, guided by the will of the Waheguru. Guru Gobind Singh thought of the *Khalsa* as his own form. He declared, "The Khalsa is God's army, guided by God's will." Now, isn't that incredibly empowering?

Both *Sikhs* and *Khalsa* follow the teachings of our Gurus. A *Sikh* who undergoes Amrit Sanchar becomes a *Khalsa* and has to wear the five Kakars. Similar to how some groups have extra responsibilities within a larger community.

You are part of something truly special: a community of brave hearts and noble souls. Just like a shining star in the night sky, you are here to spread light and goodness wherever you go.

You see, being part of the *Sikh* and *Khalsa* family is not just about what you wear or how you look. It is about the kindness in your heart, the courage in your spirit, and the goodness in your actions.

Never forget the power that lies within you. You are a *Khalsa* warrior, destined to make the world a brighter place. Keep your faith strong, your heart open, and your spirit soaring high. For you are a beacon of hope, a champion of honesty, and a true hero in the making.

Waheguru ji ka Khalsa, Waheguru ji ki Fateh!

ਅੰਮ੍ਰਿਤ ਸੰਸਕਾਰ, ਖੰਡੇ ਬਾਟੇ ਦੀ ਪਾਹੁਲ

Amrit Sanskar (FI)

Let us now get on a journey into the heart of Sikhi, where we uncover the marvels of the *Amrit Sanskar* also known as *Amrit Sanchar*. Picture it as a majestic baptismal rite, initiated by the visionary Guru Gobind Singh Ji during the vibrant festival of Vaisakhi in 1699.

When he witnessed his father, Guru Tegh Bahadur, fearlessly sacrificing his life, he understood the importance of safeguarding Sikhi and its values. That is when he took a remarkable step: he established the Khalsa - a community of courageous Sikhs who stand up for justice, just like his father did, through the *Amrit Sanchar*.

Now, brace yourself for the enchanting part: *Amrit* is no ordinary potion. It is a mystical elixir that bestows eternal uniqueness upon you. And *Sanchar*? That is when this extraordinary elixir transforms you into something truly special. You become a *Amrirtdhari* which means you have taken *Amrit*.

In days of yore, five remarkable souls known as the *Panj Pyare* were the first to taste the Amrit, igniting a tradition that continues to shine brightly today.

During this magnificent event, water, and sugar – pathasa - are blended while prayers echo in the air, stirred with the majestic Khanda sword. Sikhs aspiring to join the Khalsa and uphold the Guru's teachings partake in this awe-inspiring ceremony. Once blessed with the Amrit, they are known as the Khalsa.

Imagine yourself standing amidst a gathering of your fellow Sikhs, surrounded by the echoes of prayers and the warmth of love and devotion.

Picture yourself receiving the sacred elixir of *Amrit* that fills you with strength, purity, and unwavering faith. With each sip, you are infused with the spirit of the Khalsa - a community of fearless warriors and compassionate souls, dedicated to spreading love, justice, and harmony throughout the world.

But remember, *Amrit Sanchar* is not just about receiving blessings - it is also about embracing responsibility. As you pledge to follow the Guru's teachings and uphold the values of Sikhi, you are taking a solemn oath to be a beacon of light in a world that sometimes feels dark.

You are becoming a protector of fairness, a supporter of honesty, and a promoter of fairness. Remember, whether you are fighting unfairness, helping others, or just being kind, your actions shape the future for the better.

And when you become *Amritdhari*, you get to choose a special name! If you're a boy, you add Singh to your name, and if you're a girl, you add Kaur to your name. So, it's like having a cool new part of your name that shows everyone you are part of the Sikh family!

May your journey be filled with joy, strength, and endless blessings.

ਪੰਜ ਪਿਆਰੇ

Panj Pyare (FI)

Long ago in the lands of Panjab, there was a world where people were placed into groups called castes. These groups were like locked doors, deciding what people could do based on who their parents were. But Guru Gobind Singh Ji believed in fairness and equality for all.

He looked out upon the world and saw not just castes, but hearts full of potential. He saw siblings, all deserving of the same opportunities, regardless of where they came from or to whom they were born. So, with courage and love in his heart, Guru Ji set out to change the world.

He wanted to tear down these walls of division and build bridges of unity and equality. He wanted everyone to know that their dreams could soar as high as the sky, no matter where they started from.

How do you think he achieved this?

Well, imagine a grand festival called Vaisakhi, where the air is filled with excitement and hope. Guru Ji stands tall, calling upon Sikhs from near and far to join him at Anandpur Sahib. In a moment of daring, Guru Ji asks if anyone is willing to give up everything for him.

At first, there is silence, but then five courageous souls' step forward: Daya Ram, Dharam Das, Himmat Rai, Mohkam Chand, and Sahib Chand.

These heroes hailed from different corners of India and varied occupations. From shopkeepers to farmers, water carriers to tailors, they were all united by their love for their Guru and their readiness to serve.

With a special service called *Amrit Sanchar*, Guru Ji sealed their bond, symbolizing their unwavering loyalty to him and the Sikh faith. The *Panj Pyare* challenged the old caste system, showing that everyone is equal. They took on the prefix Singh in the names thus becoming Bhai Daya Singh, Bhai Dharam Singh, Bhai Himmat Singh, Bhai Mohkam Singh, and Bhai Sahib Singh.

Guru Ji transformed these ordinary men into warriors, anointing them as the *Panj Pyare*—the first members of the Khalsa. Their names hold special meaning, embodying qualities like kindness, righteousness, bravery, determination, and respect.

These heroes are not just names - they are beacons of light, showing us how to be our bravest, kindest, and most determined selves. They inspire us to follow their shining example, to be the heroes of our own stories, spreading kindness and respect wherever we go.

The legacy of the *Panj Pyare* continues to shine bright even today, guiding us on our spiritual journey and inspiring us to be our best selves. They are revered leaders, cherished teachers, and steadfast protectors of Sikh traditions.

So, remember Guru Ji's vision of equality. Let it inspire you to see beyond labels and differences, to treat everyone with kindness and respect. For in the tapestry of life, we are all threads woven together, each one valuable and precious.

Together, we can paint a brighter tomorrow, where every heart shines bright with the light of fairness and love.

ਪੰਜ ਕਕਾਰ

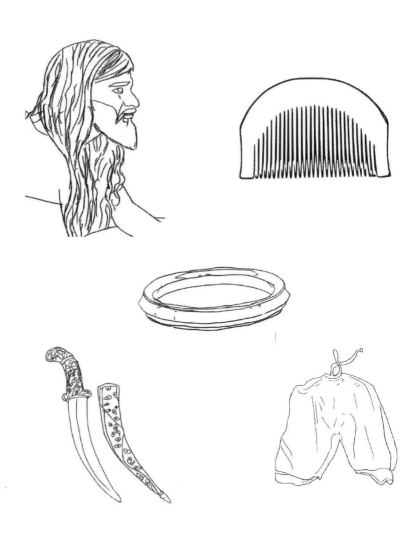

Panj Kakars (FI)

The Five Ks or the *Panj Kakars* are super cool symbols that show how much Sikhs love their faith. Are you ready to explore them? Let us go!

First up, we have *Kesh*, which means letting your hair grow naturally. It is all about staying true to yourself and embracing who you are. Sikhs believe in being real and treating everyone equally.

Next, check out the *Kanga*, a tiny comb. It is not just for keeping hair tidy, but it is also about staying clean inside and out. It is a reminder to keep your thoughts pure, and your actions disciplined.

Now, let us talk about the *Kara*, a bracelet made of strong stuff like iron. It shows how Sikhs are connected to God forever. Not unlike wearing a friendship bracelet with Waheguru and a reminder to be strong and treat everyone with respect.

And how about the *Kirpan*? It is a sword that Sikhs carry to show they are brave and ready to stand up against anything unfair and protect others. Being brave means being strong inside and standing up for what's fair and good.

Finally, there is the *Kachera*, a pair of comfy cotton underpants. Sikhs wear it to stay modest and live an honest and good life. Comfortable and ethical – what a great combo!

These Five Ks remind us to always stick to our faith and treat everyone with love and fairness.

Sikhs going through *Amrit Sanchar* have to wear the *Punj Kakar.*

Wearing the *Panj Kakars* is a big part of this promise. It is a badge of honour, showing they are proud to be Khalsa and ready to spread kindness and goodness wherever they go.

Remember, wearing the Five Ks is not about symbols but about embracing the values they represent and being proud ambassadors of Sikhi.

Embrace your *Punj Kakars* with pride and let them guide you on your journey of goodness and kindness.

You are a shining star in the Sikh community, and with the *Punj Kakars,* you can achieve anything!

ਪੰਜ ਤਖਤ

Panj Takhts (FI)

Takht in Sikhi means "throne" or "seat of authority." There are five *Takths* of worship and authority where important decisions related to Sikhi are made. They're like special places where Sikh leaders guide the community and teach important lessons.

The *Panj Takhts* are:

Akal Takht Siri Harmandir Sahib (Golden Temple): Imagine a place in Amritsar, Punjab, India, where Sikhs go to seek justice and make big decisions. Established by Guru Hargobind Sahib in 1606, It is a shining beacon of fairness, freedom, and bravery.

Takht Sri Harmandir Sahib Patna Sahib: Picture a spot in Patna, Bihar, India, where something important happened. It is where Guru Gobind Singh, the tenth Sikh Guru, was born in 1666. It reminds us of the importance of family and knowing where we come from.

Takht Sri Keshgarh Sahib: Journey to Anandpur Sahib, Punjab, India, where Guru Gobind Singh formed the Khalsa in 1699 during the Vaisakhi festival. It reminds us of bravery, justice, and doing what is right.

Takht Sri Damdama Sahib: Let us head to Talwandi Sabo, Punjab, India, where Guru Gobind Singh took a break after a big battle in 1705. This is where he finished the Guru Granth Sahib, teaching us the importance of learning and spirituality.

Takht Sri Hazur Sahib: Now, imagine a place in Nanded, Maharashtra, India, where Guru Gobind Singh's spirit joined with the Divine in 1708. It is super sacred for Sikhs and shows us the power of unwavering devotion.

And guess what? There is also a special throne for the Nihang Singhs, a unique group of Sikhs. It is like a movable symbol of their strength and spirituality, reminding them to always stand up for what is right and protect their faith.

The *Chakar Varti Takht* embodies the Nihang Singhs' dedication to spreading Sikh teachings and fostering unity among people.

All these *Takhts* stand tall as reminders of Sikh history, our values, and what it means to be part of the Sikh community. They guide us on our journey to become brave, just, and compassionate individuals, spreading light and love wherever we go.

Can you name the *Takht* in the illustration?

Keep the *Five Takhts* close to your heart and let them encourage you to be a hero, spreading love and joy wherever you go!

Let us keep exploring and learning about our rich Sikh heritage, because these *Panj Takhts* are not just places – they are symbols of our courage, justice, and love!!

ਖੰਡਾ

Khanda (FI)

The *Khanda* is not just a regular symbol; it is a badge of honour for Sikh warriors, showing off all the awesome stuff we believe in - like being truthful, fair, and strong. Let's jump in and find out why it's so amazing!

It is made up of four important parts:

The Double-Edged Sword (Khanda): Imagine a sword that has two sharp edges, like a big letter "I". This sword represents the power of truth and righteousness. It reminds Sikhs to always stand up for what's right and to fight against injustice.

The Circle (Chakra): Think of a circle like a big wheel. This circle represents the eternal nature of God, who has no beginning or end. It reminds Sikhs that God is always with them, guiding and protecting them.

The Two Swords (Kirpans): Picture two smaller swords crossed over each other. These swords represent spiritual and worldly power – Miri and Piri. They remind Sikhs to balance their spiritual life with their daily responsibilities and to always stay strong and brave.

So, when you see the Khanda, remember these three parts: the double-edged sword for truth and righteousness, the circle for God's eternal nature and the two swords for balance and strength. It's a powerful symbol that teaches important lessons for Sikhs to live by!

Remember – the *Khanda* is not just a symbol; it is our guide, showing us how to be brave and fair. Let it remind you to always stand tall, speak the truth, and spread kindness wherever you go.

Overall, the Khanda and its components hold deep spiritual and philosophical significance for Sikhs. They serve as powerful symbols that guide Sikhs in their daily lives, reminding them of their values, duties, and connection to the divine.

With love and blessings.

ਨਿਸ਼ਾਨ ਸਾਹਿਬ

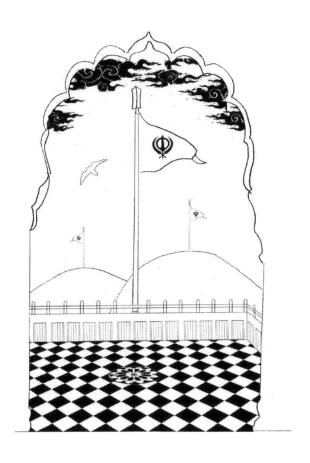

Nishan Sahib (FI)

Have you ever seen a tall, beautiful flag waving high in the air outside a Sikh gurdwara? That's called the *Nishan Sahib*, and it's not just any flag – it is a symbol of love, hope, and togetherness for Sikhs all around the world.

Imagine you're standing in front of the gurdwara, and there it is, standing tall and proud. The *Nishan Sahib* is like a big, colourful friend, welcoming everyone who comes near. It's like a beacon of light, guiding people to the sacred place where they can find peace and connection with Waheguru, the One God.

Now, let's talk about why the *Nishan Sahib* is so special. You see, every part of it has a meaning that's really important for Sikhs:

The Flag itself: It's usually saffron (orange), which represents courage and sacrifice. Sikhs are brave and always ready to help others, just like the colour orange.

The Blue Khanda: Right in the middle of the flag, there's a symbol called the Khanda. It's like a superhero emblem for Sikhs! The Khanda reminds us to stand up for what's right and to always fight against injustice. It's a sign of strength and unity.

The Pole: The pole that holds up the Nishan Sahib is like a strong tree trunk. It stands firm and tall, just like the Sikh community stands together, supporting each other through good times and bad.

The Constant Wave: Have you noticed how the Nishan Sahib always seems to be dancing in the wind? It's like it's saying, "Come, join the celebration of life!" That waving motion reminds us that life is always moving forward, and we should always keep our spirits high, no matter what.

And did you know, back in the day, during epic battles, the *Nishan Sahib* rallied our warrior ancestors, filling them with courage and reminding them of their duty to fight for justice and equality?

But here is the coolest part – the *Nishan Sahib* isn't just one colour. Once upon a time, the *Nishan Sahib* used to be blue, but then it changed to saffron, and both colours are super special.

Blue means we are strong and connected to God, and it is loved by Nihang Sikhs who keep their blue *Nishan Sahib* to honour their amazing traditions.

And get this, every Vaisakhi, we all come together to renew the *Nishan Sahib's Chola* (coverings), singing, and celebrating our devotion to our Guru. It is like throwing the coolest party ever! Have you participated in this at the Gurdwara you go to?

So, whenever you see the *Nishan Sahib*, remember that it's not just a flag – it is a symbol of love, courage, and unity for all Sikhs. It's a reminder to be strong, kind, and always stand up for what's right, just like the heroes of our faith.

ਗੁਰਦੁਆਰਾ

Gurdwara (FI)

Do you know what makes the *Gurdwara* so special? It is like the heart of our Sikhi journey, pulsating with love, wisdom, and purpose. Just like a guiding light, it leads us on a path of kindness and service.

Imagine back when Sikhi was just taking its first steps. People would gather in humble homes or under the shade of trees to worship. But as our faith flourished, the *Gurdwara* emerged as a sacred space, a sanctuary for our souls.

One of the oldest and most revered *Gurdwaras* is the Gurdwara Janam Asthan in Nankana Sahib, Pakistan, where Guru Nanak Dev Ji was born. Can you think of another sacred gurdwara in Amritsar?

Gurdwaras are like magical Swiss Army knives, offering us a plethora of blessings! They hold our precious scripture, the Guru Granth Sahib, and resonate with the melody of prayers and hymns. But they are more than just places of worship; they are havens of inclusivity where everyone is embraced with open arms.

In the *Gurdwara*, you will find stories that sparkle like gems, teaching us about courage, compassion, and the power of community. Every corner is a whisper of the tales of our ancestors' bravery and devotion, inspiring us to walk the path of virtue.

Just like a magical garden, the *Gurdwara* blossoms with the fragrance of unity and equality. It is a place where everyone is welcomed with open arms, regardless of who they are or where they come from. Here, we learn the beautiful melody of oneness, where all voices blend into one harmonious song.

The Langar hall in the *Gurdwara* is like a grand feast, where every soul is invited to partake in the joy of sharing. It is a reminder that in the eyes of Waheguru, we are all equal, and no one shall ever go hungry in our loving community.

Moreover, *Gurdwaras* are our schools, teaching us about Sikh history, values, and practices. They are our community centres, extending a helping hand to those in need through selfless service, or seva.

As you step into the *Gurdwara*, let its radiant light illuminate your path. Let its teachings guide you like a guiding star, reminding you to be kind, brave, and always ready to serve others.

Always remember that the *Gurdwara* is more than just a building. It is a beacon of light, guiding us on our Sikhi journey and reminding us to be kind, loving, and always ready to help others.

May the spirit of Sikhi dwell within your heart, filling it with endless love, courage, and joy.

ਗਿਆਨੀ

Giani (FI)

A *Giani,* also known as a Granthi, is a wise guardian of Sikh teachings, just like a champion protecting a treasure chest full of knowledge and wisdom.

Imagine a *Giani* as your guide on a magical journey through the pages of our holy scripture, the Guru Granth Sahib Ji. They help us understand its deep meanings and teachings, like a friendly storyteller sharing tales of courage, love, and faith.

But that is not all! A *Giani* is also a beacon of light in our community, spreading kindness, compassion, and positivity wherever they go. They are like a shining star illuminating the path of virtue for us to follow.

From leading prayers and ceremonies to offering wise counsel and guidance, a *Giani's* role is truly noble and awe-inspiring. They help us connect with Waheguru and strive to be better human beings each day.

A *Giani* is someone who has spent years learning about Sikh history, teachings, and scriptures. They are like treasure chests of knowledge, holding precious gems of truth and guidance.

When you meet a *Giani,* you will feel their warmth and kindness wrapping around you like a cozy blanket. They have a distinct way of making you feel safe and loved.

Listening to a *Giani's* stories is like embarking on a magical journey through time. They will tell you about the bravery of our Sikh warriors, the compassion of our

Gurus, and the importance of living a life filled with love and service.

But what makes a *Giani* truly inspirational is not just their knowledge, but their heart. They lead by example, showing us how to be kind, humble, and always willing to help others.

Cherish the moments you spend with a *Giani.* Listen to their stories, soak up their wisdom, and let their love fill your heart like sunshine on a rainy day.

For in the presence of a *Giani,* you will find not just a teacher, but a friend, a guide, and a beacon of light leading you on your Sikh journey.

Always remember to respect and honour the *Giani* in your Gurdwara. They are the guardians of our faith, the keepers of our traditions, and the pillars of our community.

ਸੰਗਤਿ

Sangat (Fl)

Let's talk about something super special in Sikhi called *Sangat*. Imagine *Sangat* as a big, cozy circle of friends and family who come together to share love, laughter, and wisdom.

You know how when you're with your friends, you feel happy and supported? Well, that's exactly what *Sangat* is all about! It's when Sikhs gather in the gurdwara or anywhere else to pray, sing, and learn together.

Now, let's discover why *Sangat* is so remarkable:

Feeling Loved and Supported: When you are part of *Sangat*, you're surrounded by people who care about you just the way you are. They cheer you on when you do something great and lift you up when you're feeling down. It's like having a big, warm hug from Waheguru!

Learning and Growing: In *Sangat*, you get to learn so many cool things about Sikhi! You listen to stories about our Gurus, sing beautiful hymns, and learn important lessons about being kind, brave, and honest. Just like having a fun classroom where you never stop growing.

Sharing and Caring: Sikhs believe in helping others, and *Sangat* is the perfect place to do that. Whether it's serving food to hungry people or lending a helping hand to someone in need, being part of sangat teaches us to be kind and caring to everyone around us.

Connecting with Waheguru: Most importantly, Sangat helps us feel closer to Waheguru, the One God. When we pray and sing together with other Sikhs, we create a special bond with Waheguru and feel His love surrounding us. It's like having a direct line to the greatest friend and protector of all!

So, always remember the magic of Sangat. It's where love grows, hearts sing, and souls shine bright. Together, we're stronger, kinder, and filled with the endless joy of Waheguru's love.

Cherish *Sangat* and let its warmth and wisdom guide you on your journey.

Keep shining bright!

ਮੱਥਾ ਟੇਕ

Matha Tek (FI)

Let us talk about something really cool called *Matha Tekna*. It's a special tradition in Sikhi that's all about showing respect and love to Waheguru and the Guru Granth Sahib Ji.

So, picture this: you're standing in front of the Guru Granth Sahib Ji, which is like our spiritual guide filled with amazing wisdom and love. When Sikhs *Matha Tekh*, it means they bow their heads to touch the ground as a sign of respect and gratitude.

Now, let's explore why Matha Tekna is so important:

Showing Respect: When we bow our heads in *Matha Tekh*, it's like saying, "Thank you, Guru Ji, for teaching us so many wonderful things!" We show respect to the Guru Granth Sahib Ji, our spiritual teacher, who guides us on the path of goodness and truth.

Humility and Gratitude: *Matha Tekna* teaches us to be humble and grateful. By lowering our heads, we show that we're ready to learn and receive the blessings of Waheguru and the Guru. You are saying, "I'm ready to listen, to learn, and to grow."

Connecting with Waheguru: When we do *Matha Tekh*, it's not just a physical action – it is a spiritual connection. We feel closer to Waheguru and the Guru Granth Sahib Ji, like they're right there with us, guiding us with their love and wisdom.

Unity and Oneness: *Matha Tekna* is something all Sikhs do together, showing that we're all equal in the eyes of

Waheguru. It doesn't matter if we're young or old, rich, or poor - we're all part of one big Sikh family, connected by our love for Waheguru and our Guru.

So, always remember the beauty of *Matha Tekna*. It's a simple but powerful way to show respect, gratitude, and love for Waheguru and our beloved Guru Granth Sahib Ji.

Keep bowing your head with a happy heart and feel the blessings of Waheguru shining down on you!

ਕੀਰਤਨ & ਕਥਾ

Kirtan and Katha (FI)

Now we are going to chat about something utterly amazing: *Kirtan, Katha,* and *Dhadis.* These are like colourful gems that sparkle in the treasure chest of Sikh traditions!

If you have ever stepped into the vibrant halls of the gurdwara, you've likely encountered the enchanting melodies of *Kirtan* and the captivating tales of *Katha.* These are magical keys that unlock the treasures of wisdom left behind by our beloved Gurus.

Picture *Kirtan* as a magnificent jam session where we join to sing or listen to hymns from the Guru Granth Sahib. It is not just music; it is a language that speaks to our souls, filling us with peace and joy.

In the days of Guru Nanak Dev Ji, the founder of Sikhi, *Kirtan* and poetry were used to impart profound spiritual lessons. Bhai Mardana Ji, Guru Nanak's faithful companion, even played the Rabab, a special instrument, during these divine sessions.

The Siri Guru Granth Sahib is composed in Ragas, each carrying its own melody and mood. When we perform *Kirtan* with the right Raga, it enhances the power of the words, taking us on a spiritual journey through music.

But *Kirtan* is not just about singing; It is a sacred path that connects us to Waheguru and to each other. It is a way to delve into the depths of Sikh philosophy and values through beautiful melodies.

Then there's *Katha*, which is like story time with a twist! It is where we dive deep into the stories and teachings of our Gurus. Through *Katha*, we learn about kindness, bravery, and the importance of being a good person. It is like unwrapping presents of wisdom, one story at a time.

And let us not forget *Dhadis*! Inspired by Guru Hargobind Ji, these lively performances keep Sikh history alive through rhythm and traditional instruments. They remind us of the brave Sikhs who came before us, inspiring us to walk the path of courage and justice.

Don't you agree that *Kirtan, Katha,* and *Dhadis* are like magical ingredients that make our Sikhi journey extra special. They fill our hearts with love, inspire us to be our best selves, and connect us to our amazing community.

So, whenever you hear the sweet melodies of *Kirtan*, the fascinating tales of *Katha,* or the thrilling beats of *Dhadis,* remember that you are part of something uniquely beautiful.

Keep listening, keep learning, and let the spirit of these traditions guide you on your Sikhi journey.

ਲੰਗਰ

Lungar (FI)

I am pretty sure you will be excited to learn more about *Langar*. Which is a big, yummy feast where everyone is invited to eat together, no matter who they are or where they come from.

This tradition goes way back to Guru Nanak Dev Ji, our first Guru, who lived over 500 years ago. He was once given some money by his father to buy goods for selling. But instead of doing that, he used it to feed hungry people he met. He believed that helping others was more important than anything else.

He got into a lot of trouble for that!

Langar is all about sharing love, kindness, and food with everyone!

Now, let's explore why Langar is so amazing:

Feeding the Heart and Soul: Langar isn't just about filling our tummies with tasty food—it's about feeding our hearts and souls with love and kindness. When we share a meal with others, we spread happiness and warmth all around.

Celebrating Equality: In *Langar*, everyone is equal. It doesn't matter if you're rich or poor, old, or young, Sikh or not - everyone sits together and eats the same food. *Langar* reminds us that we're all part of one big family, and we should treat each other with love and respect.

Serving Others with Love: Sikhs believe in helping others, and *Langar* is the perfect way to do that. Whether we're cooking, serving, or cleaning up, we do it with love and kindness, just like Guru Nanak Dev Ji taught us. *Langar* teaches us to be selfless and to care for others as much as we care for ourselves.

Spreading Happiness: Have you ever seen someone smile after taking a bite of delicious food? That's the magic of *Langar!* It brings joy to people's hearts and creates beautiful memories that last a lifetime. When we share food with others, we share happiness too!

And guess what? In *Langar,* we learn about something special called *Seva.* It means doing selfless service, like helping others without expecting anything in return. Being kind and generous is important, even without any specific reason.

Langar isn't only about food; it also offers things like medical aid, shelter, medicines, and education. It demonstrates that Sikhs are concerned about every part of a person's health and happiness.

When you visit the Gurdwara next time, why not step into the *Langar* hall and do some seva? You could lend a helping hand by serving food, passing out plates and spoons, or even offering to clean up afterward. It is an incredible opportunity to learn about humility, compassion, and love!

Always remember the beauty of *Langar.* It's more than just a meal - it is a symbol of love, equality, and kindness. Keep sharing, caring, and spreading happiness wherever you go, just like the true heroes of Sikhi!

Now let's connect some dots about what we have learned so far! Imagine the *Sikh Gurus* as the crusaders of Sikhi, guiding us on our journey towards goodness and light.

They teach us many important things, like how to be kind, truthful, and strong.

Then there is *Gurmukhi* which is a special language of love and devotion. We learn *Gurmukhi* so we can read and understand the *Siri Guru Granth Sahib Ji*, our eternal Guru. The sacred *Siri Guru Granth Sahib Ji* is our best friend, filled with wisdom and guidance from the Gurus and other wise souls.

When they are old enough and ready, some Sikhs choose to take part in the *Amrit Sanskar*. It is a special ceremony where we commit to living by the teachings of our Gurus. After this ceremony, we become part of the *Khalsa*, a community of warriors for truth and justice.

We proudly fly the Khalsa *Nishan Sahib*, a beautiful flag that represents our faith and values.

We often visit the *Gurdwara*, our spiritual home. Here, we join the *Sangat*, our Sikh family, in prayer and reflection. We show our respect by performing *Matha Tekh*, bowing our heads before the *Guru Granth Sahib Ji*.

And during *Kirtan* and *Katha*, we sing and listen to the beautiful hymns and stories of our Gurus recited by a *Giani*, filling our hearts with love and inspiration. After Ardhas, we listen to the Hukamnama and have Karah Parshad and make our way to the Lungar hall.

Langar teaches us the importance of equality and sharing. Sitting together and sharing a meal strengthens our bond as a community and reminds us of the value of selfless service.

So, you see, all these things are like pieces of a puzzle, fitting together to help us walk the path of Sikhi with love and devotion. Keep learning, growing, and spreading kindness, my young friend!

ਗੁਣ ਦੀ ਕਹਾਣੀ

Ghunn's Short Story (Fl)

I love telling stories and hope you enjoy reading it as much as I did writing it.

In the lively city of Amritsar, where the air was always filled with the delicious aroma of freshly baked kulchas and the sound of prayers echoing from the Golden Temple, there lived a young Sikh girl named Ghunn.

Her journey into Sikhi started when she was just a little girl, listening to her grandparents share stories from the Guru Granth Sahib Ji, the eternal Guru of the Sikhs.

Ghunn loved sitting with her grandmother, her eyes wide with wonder, as she listened to the verses from the Guru Granth Sahib Ji. The wisdom in those stories made her feel warm inside, like a gentle hug for her soul, making her curious to learn more about life's mysteries.

As Ghunn grew older, she learned about Miri Piri, which meant being strong and kind, just like the brave Sikh Gurus. She admired their courage and kindness, and she wanted to be like them too.

The most important day in Ghunn's journey was when she decided to take Amrit, a special ceremony where she promised to follow the teachings of Sikhi forever. It was a big step, and Ghunn felt excited and a little nervous, but she knew it was the right thing to do.

Every morning, Ghunn woke up early to pray, just like her grandparents taught her. She would then go to the Gurdwara, where she did matha tekin respect to the Guru

Granth Sahib Ji, asking for strength and guidance for the day ahead.

But Ghunn's journey wasn't just about prayers. She loved singing kirtan, the beautiful songs from the Guru Granth Sahib Ji, and listening to Katha, where she learned even more about Sikhi from wise people.

One of Ghunn's favourite parts of being Sikh was going to the Gurdwara for langar, a special meal shared by everyone. It didn't matter if you were rich or poor, everyone sat together and ate as equals, just like one big family.

As Ghunn continued her journey, she realized that being Sikh wasn't just about following rules—it was about living with love, helping others, and feeling connected to Waheguru, the divine presence that guided her every day.

And so, Ghunn's journey into Sikhi became a journey of the heart - a special adventure filled with love, kindness, and the wisdom of the Guru Granth Sahib Ji. With each step she took, she felt closer to Waheguru, knowing that she was walking the path of truth and compassion, surrounded by the love of her Sikh community.

ਨਿਤਨੇਮ

Nitnem (KP)

Nitnem is like a special treasure chest filled with powerful prayers and hymns that Sikhs recite every day to connect with Waheguru and find peace in their hearts.

Imagine this: every morning and evening, Sikhs sit down with their Nitnem prayer book and start chanting beautiful verses from Guru Granth Sahib Ji. It fills the air with love, positivity, and Waheguru's blessings!

Now, let's discover why Nitnem is so awesome:

Starting and Ending the Day with Love: When we recite *Nitnem* in the morning, we are saying, "Good morning, Waheguru! Thank you for this beautiful day." And when we recite it in the evening, we are saying, "Goodnight, Waheguru! Thank you for watching over us." *Nitnem* helps us begin and end each day with love and gratitude in our hearts.

Connecting with Waheguru: Nitnem is like a bridge that connects us to Waheguru. When we chant these sacred words, we feel Waheguru's presence all around us, guiding us, protecting us, and filling us with peace and joy. It's like having a direct line to the greatest friend and protector of all!

Finding Inner Strength: Life can be full of ups and downs, but *Nitnem* helps us stay strong and brave through it all. When we recite these powerful prayers, we fill our hearts with courage, wisdom, and kindness.

Growing in Faith and Love: Nitnem isn't just about saying words – it is about building a deep, loving relationship with Waheguru. Every time we recite these prayers, we grow closer to Waheguru and feel His endless love surrounding us. It is just like planting seeds of faith and watching them bloom into beautiful flowers of love!

Nitnem includes these *Banis* or prayers we do every day. They're like magical spells that make us feel happy and strong!

Japji Sahib: It is a morning prayer that teaches us to be humble and devoted.

Jaap Sahib: This powerful chant makes us feel brave and strong inside.

Tav-Prasad Savaiye: It is a brave song that helps us feel courageous and not scared.

Anand Sahib: This joyful song makes our hearts dance with happiness and pure joy.

Kirtan Sohila: It is like a cozy bedtime song that helps us feel thankful and peaceful as we go to sleep.

And don't forget *Chaupai Sahib!* It is like a strong shield that protects us when we need help or guidance from Waheguru. Cool, right? These prayers are like our special friends, helping us feel happy and safe every day!

So, you see, *Nitnem* is like a special treasure map that leads us to happiness, bravery, and love. It is something we do every day to fill our hearts with Waheguru's blessings and make our world a brighter place.

Always remember the magic of *Nitnem*. It's a precious gift that fills our lives with love, peace, and Waheguru's blessings. Keep chanting, keep smiling, and keep spreading Waheguru's light wherever you go!

ਅਰਦਾਸਿ

Ardhas (KP)

Ardas is like a heartfelt prayer that Sikhs say to Waheguru, the One God, to ask for blessings, guidance, and protection.

Way back, our wise Guru Gobind Singh wanted us to come together and seek Waheguru's blessings before starting something important. That's how *Ardas* came to be – a beautiful tradition that's been passed down through the generations.

Now, *Ardas* has different parts, and each one is super important. Let's explore them together:

Opening with "Ek Onkar": When we start *Ardas*, we say "Ek Onkar," which means "There is one God." It reminds us that Waheguru is the creator of everything in the universe and that we're all connected to Him.

Remembering Our Gurus: Next, we remember the ten Gurus of Sikhi. They were like superheroes who taught us how to be kind, brave, and true to ourselves. We say their names with love and gratitude for all the wisdom they shared with us.

Honouring the Guru Granth Sahib Ji: Then, we bow our heads to show respect to Guru Granth Sahib Ji, our ever-living Guru. We are saying, "Thank you, Guru Ji, for showing us the way to Waheguru's love and light."

Asking for Blessings: In *Ardas*, we ask Waheguru for blessings for ourselves, our families, and all living beings. We pray for happiness, peace, and harmony in the world.

It's like sending out wishes for everyone to be happy and safe.

Remembering Martyrs and Heroes: We also remember the brave souls who sacrificed their lives for justice and freedom. We say, "Thank you for your bravery. We will never forget you."

Ending with "Waheguru Ji Ka Khalsa, Waheguru Ji Ki Fateh": Finally, we say these powerful words, which mean "The Khalsa belongs to Waheguru, victory belongs to Waheguru." It's like shouting, "We belong to Waheguru, and with His help, we can do anything!"

So, *Ardas* is not just a prayer – it is a way for us to connect with Waheguru, remember our heroes, and spread love and kindness in the world. Keep saying *Ardas* with a happy heart and know that Waheguru is always listening and watching over you!

Keep shining bright!

ਜਪਿ, ਸਿਮਰਨ and ਸੇਵਾ

Jaap, Simran and Seva (KP)

I want to tell you about three amazing things that make Sikhi extra special: *Jaap, Simran,* and *Sewa.*

Jaap (Reciting God's Name): Imagine having a superpower that fills your heart with joy and love. That's what Jaap is all about! It's like saying "Waheguru" over and over again, like a beautiful song that makes your soul dance with happiness. When we do Jaap, we connect with Waheguru and feel His love surrounding us.

Simran (Meditating on God's Name): Simran is like a peaceful journey to Waheguru's heart. It's when we close our eyes, focus on our breath, and think about Waheguru's qualities such as love, forgiveness, compassion, and kindness. So, when you act like Waheguru by being nice to others, it is like spreading a little bit of Waheguru's love wherever you go. Simran helps us feel calm, strong, and ready to face anything that comes our way.

Seva (Selfless Service): Seva is like spreading sunshine wherever we go! It's when we help others without expecting anything in return. Whether it's feeding the hungry, helping a friend in need, or cleaning up the gurdwara, Sewa teaches us to be kind, caring, and generous. It's like planting seeds of love and watching them grow into beautiful flowers of happiness.

Now, let's talk about why *Jaap, Simran, and Sewa* are so important:

Connecting with Waheguru: Jaap, Simran, and Sewa are like magic keys that unlock the door to Waheguru's heart.

When we do them with love and devotion, we feel closer to Waheguru than ever before. It's like having a special bond with the greatest friend and protector of all!

Spreading Love and Kindness: Jaap, Simran, and *Sewa* are not just for us – they are for everyone! When we recite God's name, meditate on His love, and serve others with kindness, we spread happiness and joy wherever we go. It's like being a superhero of love, making the world a better place one smile at a time!

Becoming True Sikhs: Jaap, Simran, and *Sewa* are the heart and soul of Sikhi. They teach us to be brave, kind, and true to ourselves. When we do *Jaap, Simran,* and *Sewa* every day, we become like shining stars, lighting up the world with Waheguru's love and light.

To simplify, imagine your role model is Waheguru. *Jaap* is constantly remembering Waheguru, *Simran* is trying to be like Waheguru by being kind, compassionate, brave, and loving while *Seva* is like serving Waheguru. It is like having a secret way to always be close to Waheguru, isn't it amazing?

So, remember the magic of *Jaap, Simran,* and *Sewa*. They're not just words – they are a way of life that fills our hearts with love, joy, and Waheguru's blessings.

Keep chanting, meditating, and serving with a happy heart, and know that Waheguru is always with you, guiding you every step of the way!

ਜੋਬਨ ਦੀ ਕਹਾਣੀ

Joban's Short Story 3 (KP)

Now, young friend, because *Jaap, Simran,* and *Seva* are so important in Sikhi, here is an inspirational story that will help you along.

Once upon a time, in a bustling Sikh community, there lived a young child named Joban. Joban loved going to the Gurdwara with her family and listening to the stories from the Guru Granth Sahib Ji.

One day, while sitting in the Gurdwara, the Granthi told a story about three special friends named *Jaap, Simran,* and *Seva. Jaap* was like a magical word that made people feel happy and calm when they repeated it. *Simran* was all about thinking of all the wonderful things Waheguru did, like being kind and forgiving. And *Seva* was like being a superhero by helping others without expecting anything in return.

Joban was fascinated by these stories and wanted to learn more. So, she started practicing *Jaap* by repeating special words like "Ik Onkar" and "Waheguru" whenever she felt sad or worried. And do you know what? It really did make him feel better!

Then, Joban started doing *Simran* by thinking about how she could be kind and helpful to her friends and family. She would share his toys, help his parents with chores, and always say wonderful things to others. And guess what? Her friends started doing the same, spreading love and happiness wherever they went.

But Joban's favourite part was *Seva*. She loved the idea of being a superhero and helping others without expecting anything back. So, she joined her parents in volunteering at the community kitchen, where they served food to the hungry. She also helped her neighbours with gardening and cleaning up the park. Every act of *Seva* made her feel proud and happy inside.

As Joban grew older, she realized that *Jaap, Simran,* and *Seva* were not just stories – they were lessons to live by. They taught her to be kind, loving, and helpful to everyone around her, just like Waheguru. And from that day on, she promised to always remember the magic of *Jaap*, the goodness of *Simran*, and the power of *Seva* in her heart.

And so, the story of *Jaap, Simran,* and *Seva* lives on, inspiring many more children like Joban to be the best versions of themselves and spread love and happiness wherever they go.

Keep shining bright, and never forget that you're capable of amazing things with *Jaap, Simran,* and *Seva* by your side!

ਵੰਡ ਛਕੋ, ਨਾਮ ਜਪੋ & ਕਿਰਤ ਕਰੋ

Vand Chhako, Naam Japo and Kirat K- aro (KP)

Now let me tell you about three super amazing things that make Sikhi extra special: *Vand Chhako, Naam Japo,* and *Kirat Karo.* They are the three pillars of Sikhi.

Vand Chhako (Sharing with Others): Imagine spreading joy like confetti wherever you go that is *Vand Chhako!* It's like having a big bag of goodies and sharing them with everyone around you. Whether it's sharing food, toys, or smiles, *Vand Chhako* teaches us to be generous and kind, just like superheroes of love!

Naam Japo (Remembering God's Name): Naam Japo is like having a magical word that brings you closer to Waheguru, the One God. It is saying "Waheguru" and feeling His love wrap around you like a warm hug. *Naam Japo* teaches us to connect with Waheguru every day, no matter where we are or what we're doing. Remember Jaap and Simran?

Kirat Karo (Earning an Honest Living): Imagine doing something you love and feeling proud of it – that is Kirat Karo! It is being a superhero at school, at home, or anywhere else. Whether it's studying hard, helping your family, or being kind to others, *Kirat Karo* teaches us to do our best and be proud of who we are.

Now, let's talk about why *Vand Chhako, Naam Japo,* and *Kirat Karo* are so important:

Spreading Love and Happiness: Vand Chhako, Naam Japo, and *Kirat Karo* are like magic spells that make the world a better place. When we share with others, remember God's name, and work hard with honesty, we spread love, happiness, and Waheguru's blessings wherever we go.

Becoming True Sikhs: Vand Chhako, Naam Japo, and *Kirat Karo* are the heart and soul of Sikhi. They teach us to be brave, kind, and true to ourselves. When we live by these principles every day, we become like shining stars, lighting up the world with Waheguru's love and light.

Making Waheguru Proud: Vand Chhako, Naam Japo, and *Kirat Karo* are like a special gift we give to Waheguru. When we share, remember, and work hard with honesty, we make Waheguru smile with pride. It's like giving a big hug to the greatest friend and protector of all!

So, always remember the magic of *Vand Chhako, Naam Japo,* and *Kirat Karo.* They're not just words – they are a way of life that fills our hearts with love, joy, and Waheguru's blessings.

Keep sharing, remembering, and working hard with a happy heart, and know that Waheguru is always with you, guiding you every step of the way!

ਕੜਾਹ ਪਰਸਾਦਿ

Karah Parshad (KP)

I am sure you must have eaten warm, delicious *Karah Parshad?* Well, it is not just a tasty treat; it is big blessing from Guru Ji.

Now, *Karah Parshad* has some important parts, and each one is super awesome. Let's check them out together:

Wheat Flour, Sugar, and Ghee: Karah Parshad is made with simple ingredients - wheat flour, sugar, and ghee (clarified butter). It's like mixing up a magical potion that's full of love and sweetness. When we eat Karah Parshad, we taste the love and blessings of Waheguru!

Preparation with Love: When Sikhs make *Karah Parshad,* they do it with lots of love and devotion. It's like baking a cake for a birthday party or cooking a special meal for your family. Making *Karah Parshad* is a way to show love and kindness to everyone who eats it. Did you know that *Karh Parshad* has to be blessed with a kirpan during Ardhas before it is served to sangat?

Sharing with Everyone: One of the coolest things about *Karah Parshad* is that it's shared with everyone, no matter who they are or where they come from. It's like having a big family picnic where everyone gets to enjoy the delicious food together. *Karah Parshad* teaches us to be generous and kind to everyone around us.

Blessings from Waheguru: When we eat *Karah Parshad,* it is big hug from Waheguru. It fills us with happiness, love, and blessings from the One God. *Karah Parshad* reminds us that Waheguru is always watching over us and taking care of us, like a loving parent.

Remember the magic of *Karah Parshad*. It's not just a tasty treat – it is a symbol of love, kindness, and blessings from Waheguru. Keep sharing, eating, and spreading happiness with a happy heart, and know that Waheguru is always with you, watching over you every step of the way!

Simply put *Karah Parshad* is *Gur Kirpa*.

ਹੁਕਮਨਾਮਾ

Hukamnama (KP)

Let's explore the wonderful tradition of *Hukamnama* in Sikhi. *Hukamnama* means "command" or "order" and is like receiving a magical message from Waheguru, the One God, just for you!

Now, let's discover why Hukamnama is so amazing:

The Golden Temple: *Hukamnama* is usually taken from the Harmandir Sahib, also known as the Golden Temple in Amritsar, India. It is like receiving a letter from the most beautiful and sacred place in the world! The Golden Temple is a place of love, peace, and Waheguru's blessings.

The Siri Granth Sahib Ji: The *Hukamnama* is taken from Guru Granth Sahib Ji, our ever-living Guru. It is akin to opening a treasure chest full of wisdom, love, and guidance. The words of Guru Granth Sahib Ji teach us how to be kind, brave, and true to ourselves.

The Ardas: Before taking the *Hukamnama*, Sikhs say a special prayer called Ardas, sending a wish to Waheguru, asking for blessings, guidance, and protection. The Ardas is a way to connect with Waheguru and prepare our hearts to receive His message.

The Random Selection: When the *Hukamnama* is taken, it's like picking a lucky number out of a hat! The Giani in charge closes their eyes and opens Guru Granth Sahib Ji to a random page. Whatever message is on that page becomes the *Hukamnama* for the day.

The Message: The *Hukamnama* is like a special note from Waheguru, just for you! It is a message of love, guidance, and blessings that helps you navigate your day with courage and faith. The words of the *Hukamnama* remind us that Waheguru is always watching over us and guiding us on the right path.

Local Gurdwara: The *Hukamnama* is also taken at your local Gurdwara or your home if you are lucky enough to have Siri Guru Granth Sahib Ji in your house. A *Hukamnama* is taken by your Giani every day and on special functions like Gurpurabs, Anand Karaj or other special functions. The key is to remember that no matter the occasion, the *Hukamnama* on that day is a special message for all the Sangat to follow.

So, remember the magic of Hukamnama. It's not just a message – it is a gift from Waheguru that fills our hearts with love, wisdom, and blessings.

Keep listening, learning, and following the Hukamnama with a happy heart, and know that Waheguru is always with you, guiding you every step of the way!

Waheguru's got your back! Keep shining bright!

ੴ

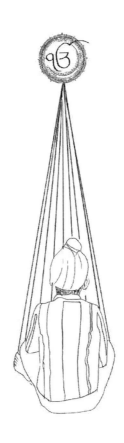

Ek OnKar (KT)

Now, let us discover why Ek Onkar is so special:

The Symbol: Ek Onkar is represented by a beautiful symbol that looks like this: "ੴ". It is a big magic wand that reminds us of something really important. The symbol is made up of two parts: "Ik" and "Onkar."

"Ik" - One God: The first part of Ek Onkar is *Ek*, which means "one." It's like saying that there's only one big boss in the universe, and that's Waheguru, the One God. Just like how there's only one sun that shines bright in the sky, there's only one Waheguru who watches over us with love and kindness.

"Onkar" - Creator of Everything: The second part of Ek Onkar is *Onkar*, which means the creator of everything. It means that Waheguru is the master artist who painted the sky, the trees, and even little you and me! Everything in the world is like a big masterpiece created by Waheguru's love and creativity.

The Unity of All: Ik Onkar reminds us that everything in the world is connected to Waheguru. It's like we're all little puzzle pieces that fit together perfectly to create one big picture. No matter who we are or where we come from, we're all part of Waheguru's big family, and we're all equally loved and cherished.

In Sikhi, we view Waheguru in two main ways: *Nirgun* and *Sargun*. *Nirgun* portrays God without any specific form or qualities that we can grasp, like the boundless expanse of the sky. Meanwhile, *Sargun* depicts God with qualities and forms that we can perceive, like the gentle breeze or the smile of a friend.

Although *Nirgun* and *Sargun* may seem different, they're intertwined, much like the waves of the ocean or the various forms of jewellery crafted from gold. The Siri Guru Granth Sahib tells us that God is both formless and with form.

Ek Onkar teaches us that we're all connected, like pieces of a puzzle. This means we should respect everyone, even if they're different from us. Kindness and understanding are important, even when we disagree.

So, remember the magic of *Ek Onkar*. It's not just a phrase – It is a reminder of the most important thing in the whole wide world: that Waheguru is the one and only creator of everything, and that we're all part of His big, beautiful masterpiece.

Keep saying *Ek Onkar* with a happy heart, and know that Waheguru is always with you, watching over you with love and kindness!

You can also do Jaap and Simran using Ek Onkar!

ਜੋਤ

Jyot (KT)

Let's explore the concept of *Jyot* or the spirit in Sikhi. *Jyot* is a shining light inside each and every one of us that makes us unique and special!

Jyot is also called *Atman*. In English it is your *Soul*.

So, imagine Waheguru as the biggest, brightest light in the whole universe. Waheguru's light is so special and amazing that it shines on everything and everyone, just like the sun shines on all the flowers and trees.

Now, here's the really cool part: every person has a tiny piece of Waheguru's light inside them. It's like having a little spark of that big, bright light right in your heart. We call this special light Jyot.

Because everyone has this *Jyot* inside them, it means that we're all connected to each other and to Waheguru. It's like we're all little pieces of a big puzzle, and when we come together, we make something really beautiful.

Now, let's discover why *Jyot* is so amazing:

The Inner Light: Jyot is like a little flame that lives inside our hearts. It is like a tiny firefly that shines bright even on the darkest nights! This light is what makes us who we are – it is what gives us our kindness, our bravery, and our love for others.

Connected to Waheguru: Jyot is like a piece of Waheguru's love that lives inside us. It is like having a little piece of the biggest, brightest star in the whole wide universe right inside our hearts! This connection to

Waheguru fills us with love, courage, and endless possibilities.

The Power of Love: *Jyot* teaches us that love is the most powerful force in the world. It's like a magic wand that can turn frowns into smiles and tears into laughter! When we let our Jyot shine bright, we spread love and happiness wherever we go.

The Importance: *Jyot* reminds us that no matter who you are or where you come from, you have a special light inside you that connects you to Waheguru and to everyone else. It's what makes us all the same and fills our hearts with love and kindness.

Remember the magic of *Jyot*. It's not just a light – it is a piece of Waheguru's love that lives inside us, guiding us, protecting us, and filling our hearts with endless joy.

So, being a Sikh is like being on a special journey. It's all about trying to get closer to something really amazing called *Jyot*. This journey of being a Sikh is like trying to get closer to that special light inside us.

We do things like praying, Jaap, Simran and Seva and learning about Waheguru to help us feel that connection even more.

It's like trying to get closer to your favourite toy or your best friend - you want to be near them because they make you feel happy and loved. That's what it is like trying to connect to *Jyot* as a Sikh.

Keep letting your *Jyot* shine bright and know that you are loved and cherished more than you could ever imagine!

ਮਨ

Maan (KT)

Imagine your *Maan*, or Mind, as the leader of your thoughts and feelings. It is like the captain of a ship, steering you through all of life's adventures. Just as a captain guides a ship through stormy seas, your *Maan* helps you navigate through challenges.

Think of your *Maan* as a treasure chest tucked away inside your heart. It holds all the things that make you special - your thoughts, your feelings, and what you believe in. It is like having your own secret room filled with important stuff.

Our Gurus teach us that having a strong *Maan* is important. It helps us make good choices and do what's right. When your *Maan* is strong, you can be kind to others, brave when things are tough, and stay focused on what really matters.

But sometimes, our minds get busy with everything happening around us. That's when we need to discipline our minds, like teaching it to stay focused on being kind, honest, and loving. It is like training a puppy to behave!

Remember, disciplining your mind or *Maan* is like going on a special journey. It takes practice and patience, just like learning something new. But with the teachings of the Gurus and the support of your parents and Sangat, you can keep your mind strong and live a life full of peace, love, and happiness.

Our Gurus call a disciplined mind *Bibaek Buddhi*. Next time you listen to the Ardhas listen for these words "*Sikhaan' noon' Sikhee daan, Kesh daan, RehT daan,*

Bibaek daan". This is a plea to Guru Sahib to bless us with a disciplined *Maan*.

Your mind is like a magical garden, waiting for you to take care of it. Fill it with the wisdom of the Siri Guru Granth Sahib. Let every word and melody guide you towards goodness and truth.

Let us join some more dots. Imagine you have five special friends: *Jyot, Jaap, Simran, Seva,* and *Maan*. Let's connect them in a simple way:

Jyot is like a bright light that guides us. *Jaap* is like saying a special word over and over again to remember something important. *Simran* is like closing your eyes and thinking about the virtues of Waheguru.

Seva is like doing something nice for others, like helping your friends or family. And Maan is like feeling proud and happy about who you are and what you believe in.

So, *Jaap* helps us remember, *Simran* helps us connect with what's important, *Seva* helps us show love to others, and when we practice *Jaap, Simran,* and *Seva,* our *Maan* becomes disciplined, strong, and wise. It helps us make good choices and spread love and happiness wherever we go.

And by doing this we connect to our *Jyot!*

They're all connected, like pieces of a beautiful puzzle that make our Sikh way of life special and meaningful.

ਹੁਕਮਿ

Hukam (KT)

Hukam is a magical map created by Waheguru, guiding us to happiness and peace. *Hukam* whispers softly, "Every happening has a purpose, all part of a beautiful design!"

Life can be like a dance, with twists and turns, but we trust that it is all part of Waheguru's plan, even if we don't always understand why. *Hukam* teaches us to flow with life's rhythms, knowing that peace awaits us.

Now, let's discover why Hukam is so amazing:

The Divine Plan: Hukam is like a big map that Waheguru has created for us. It shows us the path we're supposed to take in life, filled with adventures, challenges, and lots of love! Just like how your favourite storybook has a beginning, middle, and end, *Hukam* guides us on our journey through life.

Trusting Waheguru: Hukam teaches us to trust Waheguru with all our heart. It's like having a big, strong protector watching over us, making sure everything happens just the way it's supposed to. Even when things don't go exactly as we planned, we know that Waheguru has a bigger plan for us - one filled with love and blessings.

Living in the Moment: Hukam reminds us to live in the present moment and enjoy every second of our adventure. It's like being on a rollercoaster ride - sometimes it's scary, sometimes it's exciting, but it's always an amazing journey! When we trust *Hukam*, we can let go of worries about the future and just focus on being happy right now.

Accepting What Is: Hukam teaches us to accept things just the way they are. It's like when you're playing a game and you have to follow the rules - even if you don't win every time, you still have fun! When we accept *Hukam*, we can be at peace knowing that everything is happening for a reason, and that Waheguru is always by our side.

But recognizing *Hukam* is like finding clues in a treasure hunt. Here's how you can do it:

Listen to Your Heart: Sometimes, you might feel a little whisper inside you, guiding you in the right direction. That's *Hukam*! It's like having a little friend inside you, helping you make good choices.

Look for Signs: Sometimes, Waheguru sends us little signs to show us the way. It could be a beautiful rainbow after a rainy day or a friendly smile from a stranger. These signs are like little hints from Waheguru, telling us that everything is going to be okay.

Pay Attention to Your Feelings: When something feels right in your heart, that's *Hukam*! It's like when you're playing a game, and you know exactly what to do without even thinking about it. Trusting your feelings is a great way to recognize *Hukam*.

Talk to Waheguru: You can talk to Waheguru just like you talk to your best friend. Share your hopes, dreams, and worries, and listen for Waheguru's response. Sometimes, it might come as a feeling of peace or a sense of calmness in your heart.

Remember, recognizing *Hukam* is all about listening, watching, and feeling with your heart. Keep trusting yourself and Waheguru, and you'll always find your way!

Think of *Hukam* as the universe's gentle guidance, leading us every step of the way. It is not just about rules; It is about seeing how everything is connected.

Just like a river flows effortlessly along its course, *Hukam* encourages us to go with the flow of life, embracing each moment with grace and gratitude.

Let us now connect *Jyot* and *Hukam.*

The connection between *Jyot* and *Hukam* is like a special bond between your inner light and the divine plan of Waheguru.

Jyot, or the inner light, is the spark of Waheguru's presence within you. It's that feeling of warmth, love, and intuition that guides you in life. When you listen to your Jyot, you're tuning into the wisdom and guidance of Waheguru that resides within you.

Hukam, on the other hand, is Waheguru's divine plan for the universe. It's like the big picture, the grand design that encompasses everything. *Hukam* guides the flow of life, shaping events and experiences according to Waheguru's will.

Now, the beautiful connection between *Jyot* and *Hukam* is that when you listen to your inner light, you're aligning yourself with Waheguru's plan. Your *Jyot*, your intuition, your inner wisdom - they're all part of the divine guidance that leads you on the path set by *Hukam.*

In simpler terms, when you listen to your *Jyot*, you're following *Hukam*. You're walking the path that Waheguru has laid out for you, guided by the light of your own inner divinity. And when you trust in that connection, you find peace, purpose, and fulfilment in life.

But how do you listen to your *Joth*? Here's how you can do it:

Be Still: Find a quiet and peaceful place where you can sit comfortably without any distractions.

Close Your Eyes: Close your eyes and take a few deep breaths. Try to relax your body and clear your mind of any thoughts.

Focus Inward: As you sit quietly, focus your attention on your heart. Imagine a warm, glowing light shining brightly inside you. This is your *Jyot*.

Listen: Listen to your heart and feelings. Notice how you're feeling and what thoughts come to mind. Your *Jyot* may communicate with you through your intuition, feelings, or inner knowing.

Trust Yourself: Trust that whatever you feel, or sense is important and valid. Your *Jyot* is always there to guide you and help you make good choices.

Act with Love: Once you've listened to your *Jyot*, follow its guidance with love and kindness. Trust that your inner light will always lead you in the right direction.

Remember, listening to your Jyot is like listening to your best friend inside you. Trust yourself, trust your feelings, and trust that your *Jyot* will always guide you with love and wisdom.

ਮਾਇਆ

Maya (KT)

Think of *Maya* like a tricky magician who tries to distract us from what really matters – our connection with Waheguru and finding peace inside ourselves.

It is like playing a game where things look real but are just make-believe. *Maya* might make us think that having tons of toys or cool stuff will make us super happy, but real happiness comes from love, kindness, and feeling calm inside.

Sometimes, *Maya* makes us feel jealous or want things we don't really need. It is like a puzzle trying to confuse us and lead us away from doing what's right.

Imagine you're in a desert, and you spot something that seems like a pool of water in the distance. But as you get closer, you realize it's not really water; it's just a trick caused by the light and heat. That's *Maya*, playing tricks on your eyes.

Or think about when you're dreaming – everything feels so real, but then you wake up and realize it was all in your head. That's *Maya*, making you believe something that isn't true.

Even cool stuff like virtual reality or magic tricks can trick us into thinking something is real when it is not. *Maya* likes to mess with our senses!

And it is not just about what we see or feel – *Maya* can also sneak into our minds in other ways, like making us too attached to stuff we own, or making us think we're better than others.

But here's the cool part – our Gurus have given us guidance to see through *Maya's* tricks! They teach us to focus on stuff that's important – like being nice to others, helping people out when they need it, and knowing that Waheguru is always there for us.

So, next time you feel *Maya* trying to trick you, remember to stay grounded in love, kindness, and what our Gurus taught us. If you stick to what's important, you can beat *Maya's* tricks and find true happiness inside yourself.

Now, let's talk about *Maan* and *Maya*. *Maya* tries to trick your *Maan* into wanting things that might not be good for you. But guess what? Your *Maan* disciplined by Guru's teachings, is super smart, thanks to your Guru! It helps you see through *Maya's* tricks and focus on what really matters – like being kind and loving.

So, my impressive friend, listen to your disciplined *Maan* and don't let *Maya* fool you. Stick to what's important, and you'll shine bright like a star!

You're amazing!

ਕਰਮਾ

Karma (KT)

Karma is like a secret superpower we all have. Imagine you're playing a big game where every choice you make is like magic, shaping your life. Cool, right?

Our amazing Gurus teach us that what we do really matters. They say it is all part of a special plan by Waheguru.

Think of *Karma* like you are planting seeds in a garden. If you plant seeds of kindness by helping others and being nice, you'll grow flowers of joy. But if you plant seeds of meanness, you'll grow weeds that make things hard.

But here's the awesome part: You get to choose what kind of seeds you plant every day! By doing good things, you make the world a better place and bring happiness to yourself too. It is like throwing a boomerang - the good stuff comes back to you!

So, always try to be kind and loving. Your actions have the power to change the world!

Now, let's talk about three important things in our Sikh journey: *Maan, Maya,* and *Karma*.

A disciplined *Maan* is like your inner compass, guiding you through life. *Maya* is tricky - it makes us want things we don't really need. And *Karma* is like a special recipe - what we do comes back to us.

But if we have a disciplined *Maan*, we can see through *Maya's* tricks and make good choices. When we do good things, we make good *Karma*, bringing happiness and blessings.

Recall, what you do comes back to you like a boomerang. So, let's make the world brighter together with our charitable deeds!

Remember, my friend, keep your *Maan* strong, and don't let *Maya* trick you! You're amazing just the way you are!

Lots of love and encouragement.

ਗੁਰ ਪਰਸਾਦਿ

Gurprasad (KT)

Gurprasad is like getting a big, amazing gift from Waheguru, the One God, and it's filled with love, blessings, and magic! Simply put it means "with the grace of the Guru" or "by the favour of the Guru".

Let's talk about why we need *Gurprasad*, or the grace of the Guru, to understand and follow Gurbani.

Imagine you have a really special Guru, the Guru Granth Sahib Ji, filled with amazing stories and secrets. Gurbani in the SGGS, is written by our Gurus. But sometimes, the words can be a little tricky to understand, like a puzzle that's hard to solve.

That's where *Gurprasad* comes in! It's like having a wise friend who helps you understand the Gurbani and shows you how to live its lessons in your everyday life. When we ask for *Gurprasad,* we're asking for the Guru's guidance and blessings to help us understand Gurbani and follow its teachings.

Just like how a lantern lights up a dark room, *Gurprasad* lights up our minds and hearts, helping us see the true meaning behind the words of Gurbani. With *Gurprasad,* we can understand how to be kind, brave, and true Sikhs, following the path set by our Gurus.

When we say our prayers and thank Guru Ji, we are expressing thanks for all the good stuff and asking for help when we need it. *Gurprasad* and its cousin *Gurkirpa* are like reminders of how much the Guru loves us, and they help us be kind and humble.

Guru Gobind Singh also uses *Tav Prasad* which means "with Waheguru's blessings".

So, always remember to ask for *Gurprasad* when you read or hear Gurbani. With the Guru's grace, you'll find wisdom, strength, and love to guide you on your journey as a Sikh.

Keep learning, keep growing, and know that the Guru is always by your side, helping you every step of the way!

You've got this!

ਵਾਹਿਗੁਰੂ

Waheguru (KT)

Let's dive into the amazing world of *Waheguru* and discover why He's so special to us!

Waheguru is made up of two special words: *Wahe*, which means "Wonderful" or "Great," and *Guru*, which means teacher or guide. Talking to *Waheguru* is akin to conversing with an amazing teacher who helps us understand the world.

Imagine *Waheguru* as the biggest, kindest, and most loving protector in the whole wide universe. He's like the sun that shines bright, warming our hearts with His love and light.

Now, let's talk about some of Waheguru's super cool qualities:

Love, Love, Love: Waheguru is all about love! His love is like a big, warm hug that wraps around us, making us feel safe, happy, and super loved.

Wisdom Galore: Waheguru knows everything - like the smartest teacher you've ever met! His wisdom helps us learn and grow, guiding us on the right path in life.

Always There for Us: Waheguru is like our best friend who's always there for us, no matter what. Whenever we need help or feel scared, He's right by our side, cheering us on and giving us strength.

Making Dreams Happen: Waheguru can do anything! He's like a magician who makes dreams happen every day. From blooming flowers to twinkling stars, everything around us is a magical gift from *Waheguru*.

Getting to know *Waheguru* is like making a new friend. Here's how you can do it:

Talk to Waheguru: Just like you talk to your friends, you can talk to Waheguru too! Tell Him about your day, your dreams, and even your worries. You can talk to Him anytime, anywhere—*He's always listening!*

Listen for His Voice: *Waheguru* might not talk back in words, but He speaks to us in other ways. Sometimes, He sends us little signs, like a beautiful rainbow after a rainy day or a friendly smile from a stranger. Keep your eyes and ears open for these special messages from Waheguru!

Feel His Love: *Waheguru's* love is all around us, like a big, warm blanket wrapping us up. You can feel His love in your heart, especially when you're doing things that make you happy and help others. That warm, fuzzy feeling? That's *Waheguru* giving you a big hug!

Read Gurbani: Gurbani is like a special letter from Waheguru, filled with His wisdom and love. When you read or listen to Gurbani, you're getting to know Waheguru better and learning how to be a good Sikh.

Keep doing *Jaap, Simran, Seva* and your *Nitnem* and you will get to know Waheguru.

Remember, getting to know *Waheguru* is like building a friendship - it takes time, patience, and lots of love. Keep talking to Him, listening for His voice, feeling His love, and reading Gurbani, and you'll grow closer to *Waheguru* with each passing day.

And always remember, *Waheguru* loves you more than you could ever imagine! Do not forget to be grateful and say *Gurkirpa!* With these powerful words, you're spreading magic everywhere you go!

ਹੰਕਾਰ

Haumai (KT)

Our Gurus call our ego *Haumai* or *Hanker*. So, what is it? Well, it is when we feel super proud or think we're better than others. It's like our ego is trying to steal the spotlight!

Sikh teachings tell us about five things that can trip us up on our journey to feeling close to Waheguru and being good people. They're Desire, Anger, Greed, Attachment, and our buddy *Haumai*.

Haumai might sound like a big word, but it is really about something we all deal with. It is like a sneaky voice inside us that tries to make us feel like we're better than others.

But do you know what? We're all equally special in Waheguru's eyes. *Haumai* might try to make us feel big, but true greatness comes from being humble, kind, and caring towards others.

Don't worry! Our Gurus give us everything we need to beat *Haumai* and find spiritual freedom. Find that special treasure inside you (your *Jyot*) and tell your ego to take a break so you can follow Waheguru's plan (*Hukam*).

Our Gurus teach us that being humble, helping others, and being kind are powerful ways to fight our ego. And when we let go of our pride, amazing things happen - we make our communities happier and more peaceful.

In our Sikh way of life, we keep things simple and stay humble. We find joy in sharing meals together (*langar*) and helping others without expecting anything in return (*seva*). So, remember, by connecting with Waheguru and helping others, we can beat *Haumai* and feel connected to the wonder around us.

Here's a secret tip: When someone compliments you and you start feeling proud, just say *Gurkirpa*! It is like saying, "It is not just me - It is my Guru's blessings!"

Ok friend, now let us connect some dots: *Waheguru, Gurparsad, Gurbani, Hukam, Jyot, Maya,* and *Haumai.*

First off, *Waheguru* is like the big boss of everything, the one who made the entire world and all of us. It is like having a super loving and caring friend who's always there for us.

Now, *Gurparsad* is Guru's grace. With Guru's grace we understand and unlock the wisdom of *Gurbani* and learn the secrets of recognising our *Jyot and* Guru's *Hukam.*

But then, there's *Maya. Maya* is a bit tricky. It is the same as when you see something shiny and cool, and you really, really want it, even if you don't really need it. *Maya* makes us want things that might not be important and forget about what's truly special.

And finally, there's *Haumai. Haumai* is when we start feeling too proud or think we're better than others. It is the same as when you win a game and start showing off to everyone. *Haumai* tries to make us forget that Waheguru is the one who gives us all the good stuff.

So, here's the deal: *Waheguru* gives us *Gurparsad* because *Waheguru* loves us so much. But sometimes, *Maya* and *Haumai* try to get in the way. *Maya* makes us want things we don't need, and *Haumai* makes us feel too proud.

The important thing is to remember that everything good comes from *Waheguru's* love. When we stay humble and grateful, we can see through *Maya* and *Haumai* and focus on what really matters - our connection with *Waheguru*.

So, let's always be thankful for *Gurparsad* and remember that *Waheguru's* love is the most important thing of all.

Hope that helps! You've got this!

ਗੁਰਬਾਣੀ & ਜਗਤ

Gurbani and Creation (KT)

As we continue our journey of exploration and learning, let us now explore *Gurbani* and the tale of creation.

Picture *Gurbani* as a precious gem nestled within Siri Guru Granth Sahib Ji, brimming with wisdom and love from our Sikh Gurus and enlightened souls from everywhere.

Gurbani, which means "the words of the Guru," is like a timeless map that shows us the way forward. It is full of smart ideas from our Sikh Gurus and other wise folks, teaching us how to live our best lives.

Gurbani becomes even more extraordinary because it is accompanied by musical melodies known as Ragas. When we sing or recite it, it feels like our souls are dancing with joy! This musical part makes our journey even more exciting and helps us feel closer to Waheguru.

Covering all kinds of important stuff, *Gurbani* tells us to love Waheguru, be nice to others, fight for fairness, treat everyone the same, stay humble, and know ourselves better. These ideas are for everyone, no matter who they are.

Now, let's talk about how everything began. *Gurbani* says that before anything else, there was only Waheguru, chilling out peacefully. Then, with a special word the universe was born in a big explosion! It is like Waheguru painted a beautiful picture, and everything came to life.

Okay, let's break it down. Imagine there's this super special Creator, called *Ek*. *Ek* is like the best parent ever, watching over everything. *Gurbani* says every little thing, from tiny ants to huge galaxies, is all part of *Ek's* big plan. *Ek* is *Waheguru*.

When we say *Ek is Waheguru*, it is like saying "Waheguru is the one and only big chief in charge of everything, like the top boss of all bosses!" It's sort of like having the most important leader ever taking care of everything.

Ok, now back to our story. Before everything else, *Ek* was just chilling in a peaceful meditation. Then, with a magical word, *OnKar*, boom, the universe came alive! And ever since, *Ek* has been taking care of everything with lots of love, just like a parent.

When we say our Guru Granth Sahib starts with *Ek OnKar*, it's means that it all began with Waheguru. It's the very first line of our Mool Mantar, which is like the foundation of our beliefs.

It tells us that Waheguru is the one who started everything, like the very first spark that made the whole universe. So, SGGS Ji reminds us that everything comes from Waheguru.

Isn't that amazing? Understanding how everything began helps us see how formidable and diverse the world is. We realize we're all part of something big.

Throughout our journey together, we've discovered that everything in the world is linked, much like pieces of a colossal puzzle. *Gurbani* enlightens us on living with love, kindness, and compassion, all guided by an amazing plan known as *Hukam*.

When we look around and see all the impressive things in the world, it is like going on a big adventure! We're discovering how everything fits together perfectly, like a magical dance of harmony.

Let *Gurbani* be your guide as you explore the wonders of creation. Let it inspire you to marvel at the universe and to live each day with love, kindness, and thanks. Keep shining bright.

ਮੂਲ ਮੰਤਰ

ੴ ਸਤਿ ਨਾਮੁ ਕਰਤਾ
ਪੁਰਖੁ ਨਿਰਭਉ ਨਿਰਵੈਰੁ
ਅਕਾਲ ਮੂਰਤਿ ਅਜੂਨੀ
ਸੈਭੰ ਗੁਰ ਪ੍ਰਸਾਦਿ ॥

Mool Mantar (KT)

The *Mool Mantar* is like a powerful magic spell that fills our hearts with courage and love. *Mool* means "the root" or "fundamental" and *Mantar* means "the formula". So *Mool Mantar* is the "fundamental formula" or "fundamental statement" to understanding Gurbani.

It is the first verse in Siri Guru Granth Sahib, our special guidebook for life.

Here's what it says:

੧ੳ ਸਤਿ ਨਾਮੁ ਕਰਤਾ ਪੁਰਖੁ ਨਿਰਭਉ ਨਿਰਵੈਰੁ ਅਕਾਲ ਮੂਰਤਿ ਅਜੂਨੀ
ਸੈਭੰ ਗੁਰ ਪ੍ਰਸਾਦਿ ॥

*Ek-Onkar Sat Naam Karta Purakh Nirbhau-Nirvair Akaal
Murat Ajooni Saibhang Gurparsad.*

"There's only one God, and this God is super truthful, made everything, isn't scared of anything, doesn't do hate, lives forever, doesn't need anyone else to exist, and thanks to our Guru's blessing, we know all about it!"

Isn't that amazing? It is like having a champion friend who's always there for us, teaching us how to be brave and kind.

Emulating the *Mool Mantar* at any age is super exciting and important. Here's how you can do it:

Spread love and kindness like "Ek Onkar": Treat everyone with love and kindness, just like Waheguru loves us all equally. Be a good friend and help others whenever you can.

144

Be truthful like "Sat Naam": Always tell the truth, even if it is hard. Being honest with yourself and others makes you a trustworthy and dependable friend.

Respect and appreciate creation like "Karta Purakh": Treat the world and everything in it with respect. Appreciate the beauty of nature and take care of the environment.

Be brave and fearless like "Nirbhau": Don't let fear stop you from trying new things or standing up for what's right. Be brave like a lion and face challenges with courage.

Live without hate like "Nirvair": Let go of anger and hatred. Instead, forgive others and spread love wherever you go. Be a peacemaker and a friend to everyone.

Remember Waheguru's eternal love like "Akaal Murat": Know that Waheguru's love is always with you, guiding you through life's difficulties. Trust in Waheguru's plan for you and stay positive.

Stay connected to Waheguru like "Ajooni Saibhang": Keep your faith strong and stay connected to Waheguru through prayers and meditation. Trust in Waheguru's wisdom and guidance.

Seek wisdom from the Guru like "Gurparsad": Listen to the teachings of your Guru and follow their guidance. Learn from their wisdom and strive to be the best version of yourself.

By emulating the *Mool Mantar,* you'll grow up to be a kind, brave, and loving person, just like Waheguru wants us to be. You've got this!

ਨਾਮ

Naam (KT)

Naam. It is like having a magical key that unlocks the power of God's name, filling our hearts with the special essence of Waheguru all around us.

Naam means remembering Waheguru all the time, just like you remember your favourite superhero or cartoon character. It's like having their name in your heart and mind, and whenever you think of them, you feel happy and safe. Remember what we said about *Jaap* and *Simran*?

So, for Sikhs, *Naam* is about always thinking of Waheguru and feeling happy and peaceful because of it.

When we say *Naam*, we are calling out to our best friend, the one who's always there for us. Can you feel how special that is? Imagine having a special code that lets you connect with something amazing!

Naam is super important for us Sikhs because it helps us get closer to God and feel spiritually free. It is like going on an incredible adventure every time we think about it or say it out loud.

Imagine *Naam* as a big, warm hug for our minds. It helps us become better people, making us humble, kind, and letting go of things that don't matter.

Naam shows us that we're all connected to God, no matter who we are or where we come from. And when we think about *Naam,* we can break free from all the stuff that holds us back and feel genuinely happy inside.

Now, let's talk about *Naam's* buddies: *Shabad* and *Waheguru*. They're like a special team, working together to make our bond with the Divine super strong.

Shabad is like a magical song we find in our Siri Guru Granth Sahib Ji. It teaches us all about Waheguru and how to be kind and loving.

And *Waheguru*? Well, that's the big boss, the amazing Creator of everything! When we say Waheguru, it is like giving a big shout-out to God and feeling their love all around us.

So, *Naam, Shabad,* and *Waheguru* are like the ultimate dream team. *Naam* connects us to God, *Shabad* teaches us about God, and *Waheguru* is the one we're talking to! Together, they help us feel close to God and lead lives filled with love and goodness.

Isn't that impressive? Keep saying *Naam*, listening to *Shabad*, and shouting out to *Waheguru*, and you'll always feel their love with you!

So, remember, *Naam* isn't just a word; It is a unique way to connect with God, filling us with love, gratitude, and devotion. Let's keep shining brightly on this amazing journey of life, following the path of love and service taught by our Guru.

You're truly magnificent! Keep shining your light!

ਚੜ੍ਹਦੀ ਕਲਾ

Chardikala (KT)

Chardikala is all about staying positive and optimistic, no matter what challenges come our way. Isn't that extraordinary?

Imagine yourself as a sturdy tree, standing tall with courage and kindness, even when things get tough. That's exactly what *Chardikala* is all about! It is like having a sunny outlook on life, just like the sun that keeps shining bright no matter what.

At the heart of *Chardikala* is a strong belief in Waheguru's plan, which we call *Hukam*. It means we see challenges as chances to grow closer to God and become even stronger.

Living with *Chardikala* means facing life's tricky problems with a big smile, holding onto bravery, happiness, hope, and positivity. Even in the darkest times, we believe that brighter days are ahead.

So, *Chardikala* is akin to having a magic wand that spreads happiness to everyone around us. It fills our hearts with excitement and curiosity, just like solving puzzles or learning new things.

And when tough times come knocking, *Chardikala* helps us stay strong and never give up. It is like a guiding light, showing us that everything will be okay because it is all part of Waheguru's plan.

Imagine you're a brave warrior, facing challenges with a big smile and a heart full of courage. That's what

Chardikala is! It is staying hopeful and happy, even when things seem tough.

Here's some guidance from our Gurus on how to stay in *Chardikala:*

Nanak Naam Chardi Kala, Tere Bhane Sarbat Da Bhala: This line from Ardhas teaches us to remember Waheguru's name and always remain in high spirits, wishing well for everyone.

Satguru Ki Sewa Safal Hai, Je Ko Kare Chit Laye: Serving others and helping those in need makes our lives fruitful and brings joy. So, always be ready to lend a helping hand to others.

Rab Rakha, Khalsa Ji Anek: Trust that Waheguru is always looking after you, and as a member of the Khalsa, you are part of a larger family that cares for each other.

Guru Granth Sahib Ji De Path te Kirtan Vich Dhyan Lagao: Listening to and understanding the teachings of Guru Granth Sahib Ji and singing the praises of Waheguru helps keep your mind peaceful and happy.

Hukam Razai Chalna, Nanak Likhyana Lekh: Trust in Waheguru's divine will and accept whatever comes your way with grace, knowing that it's all part of Waheguru's plan.

Kirat Karni, Naam Japna, Vand Chakna: Work hard, remember Waheguru's name, and share with those in need. These are the foundations of a Sikh's life and lead to a state of Chardikala.

Remember, staying in *Chardikala* doesn't mean you won't face difficulties, but it means facing them with a positive attitude, faith in Waheguru, and the teachings of the Sikh Gurus.

Remember, *Chardikala* is like a special power that comes from *Naam, Shabad,* and *Waheguru.*

Chardikala is not about how full your glass is. *Chardikala* implies your glass is always overflowing!

Stay hopeful, stay positive, and never give up. With *Chardikala* by your side, you can overcome any challenge and achieve wonderful things.

You have got this!

ਸਰਬੱਤ ਦਾ ਭਲਾ

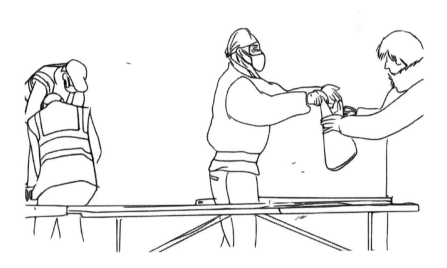

Sarbat da Bhalla (KT)

Imagine a beautiful garden filled with colourful flowers, where each flower is unique and special in its own way. Now, think of our world as this vast garden, with people from all walks of life, just like those flowers.

Sarbat da Bhalla is like the sunshine that kisses every flower in the garden, making them bloom and shine. It means wishing well for every single person in this world, just like we want happiness and goodness for ourselves.

For Sikhs, *Sarbat da Bhalla* means treating everyone with fairness and caring for them, no matter who they are. We are not just saying kind words but promising to live in a way that shows love, kindness, and happiness to everyone we meet. Being there for others and helping them, just like we would want someone to help us.

And do you know what? By spreading *Sarbat da Bhalla*, we're making the world a better place for everyone. We're showing how important it is to treat others with respect and fairness, just like our Guru taught us.

Now, let's connect some dots in our puzzle: *Ardas, Chardikala, Naam, Shabad, Waheguru,* and *Sarbat da Bhalla!*

Ardas is like a special prayer that we say to Waheguru. It is a way for us to talk to God and ask for blessings for ourselves and everyone else.

When we say *Ardas,* we're filled with *Chardikala,* which means staying positive and strong no matter what. It is like having a bright light inside us that never goes out, even when things get tough.

And speaking of positivity, *Chardikala* connects to *Naam, Shabad,* and *Waheguru*. *Naam* is like our special connection to God, *Shabad* is the beautiful song in our Siri Guru Granth Sahib that teaches us about God, and *Waheguru* is the amazing Creator of everything.

When we remember *Naam*, listen to *Shabad,* and say *Waheguru*, it fills our hearts with happiness and helps us stay positive with *Chardikala*.

But wait, there's more! There's also *Sarbat da Bhalla,* which is all about spreading happiness and kindness to everyone, just like we ask for in *Ardas*. It is sharing a big smile and a helping hand with everyone around us.

So, you see, all these things are connected. When we say *Ardas*, we're filled with *Chardikala*, which comes from remembering *Naam, Shabad, and Waheguru*. And with *Chardikala*, we spread *Sarbat da Bhalla* to make the world a better place for everyone.

So, when you hear *Sarbat da Bhalla*, remember that you have the power to spread happiness and kindness everywhere you go, just like the sunshine makes the garden flourish. And by doing so, you're not just making the world a better place for others, but also for yourself.

Isn't that amazing? Keep saying your prayers, staying positive, and spreading kindness, my little friend. You're making an enormous difference in the world!

ਆਨੰਦ

Anand (KT)

Anand means 'happy' *or* 'joyful'. *Anand* is a magical gift of happiness and joy that comes from being close to Waheguru. It is comparable to when you feel so happy and content, like your heart is smiling all the time.

You know that feeling when you're surrounded by love, and everything just feels right. That's *Anand!*

Imagine you're walking in a beautiful garden full of roses. When you get close to a rose, you can smell its sweet fragrance all around you. It's like a hug for your nose, making you feel happy and calm.

Now, think of *Anand* like the fragrance of a rose, but for your heart and soul. Just like how the smell of a rose makes you feel good, *Anand* fills your heart with joy and peace. It is a warm, cozy feeling that spreads inside you, making you smile from the inside out.

So, just like you enjoy the smell of roses in a garden, you can also enjoy *Anand* by doing things that make you feel happy, being kind to others, and connecting with Waheguru. It is as if you're spreading the lovely aroma of happiness everywhere you go!

But most importantly, remember that *Anand* comes from within. So, always keep your heart pure, your mind focused on Waheguru, and spread love and kindness wherever you go. That way, you'll always be surrounded by anand!

Now, let's connect a few more dots between *Mool Mantar, Shabad, Waheguru, Naam, Chardikala, Sarbat da Bhalla, and Anand.*

Mool Mantar is like the opening melody of a beautiful song. It sets the stage for everything that follows in Sikh teachings. It tells us about *Waheguru*, our wonderful Creator, and how amazing and loving they are.

Shabad is like the lyrics of that song. It is the beautiful words and teachings we find in our holy Guru Granth Sahib Ji. When we read or listen to *Shabad*, it fills our hearts with wisdom and guidance from *Waheguru*.

Now, *Naam* is like the rhythm of that song. It is the special connection we have with Waheguru. When we say or think about *Naam*, it is like tuning into a radio station that plays nothing but love and positivity.

And when we repeat *Waheguru*'s name, it fills us with *Chardikala* - that is like a superpower of staying positive and strong, no matter what challenges come our way.

Sarbat da Bhalla is like the chorus of that song. It is all about spreading happiness and kindness to everyone, just like we want for ourselves. When we help others and treat them with respect, it is like adding beautiful harmony to the world.

And guess what happens when we put all these things together? We feel *Anand* - that is like a big burst of joy and happiness in our hearts.

It is like swaying to the melody of *Mool Mantar*, singing the lyrics of *Shabad*, and feeling the rhythm of *Naam*, all while spreading love with *Sarbat da Bhalla* and staying strong with *Chardikala*.

So, remember this beautiful connection. Let *Mool Mantar* be your guide, *Shabad* be your inspiration, *Naam* be your strength, *Chardikala* be your armour, *Sarbat da Bhalla* be your mission, and *Anand* be your reward. !

ਅਨੰਦ ਕਾਰਜ

Anand Karaj (KT)

Ask your mom and dad about their *Anand Karaj!* Have you ever been to one?

In Sikhi, instead of calling them "ceremonies," we use the word *Karaj* for our extraordinary events. *Karaj* means "action" or "act" in Punjabi, showing how lively and dynamic our traditions are. *Anand*, as you now know, means happiness or bliss.

So, *Anand Karaj* is a magical event where two people decide to start a new journey and family with Waheguru's blessings. Sangat gathers around to celebrate the *Anand Karaj* at the Gurdwara.

In the past, when our parents arranged our marriages, it felt like a massive surprise! We did not have the chance to meet our future spouse until the actual wedding day arrived. Can you believe it?

Just imagine meeting your new best friend at a party and intuitively knowing you will be friends forever! But hey, no giggling! That is just how things were in those days!

Long ago, our fourth Sikh Guru, Guru Ram Das Ji, added something remarkable to the *Anand Karaj*. He wrote down four special verses called the *Laavaan*. Each *Laavaan* is a step in a beautiful journey.

By reciting *Laavaan,* we draw nearer to our Guru, who blesses us with Anand – a feeling of complete happiness and satisfaction.

Now let us connect some dots.

Imagine *Guru* as our wise and loving teacher, who shows us how to be kind and brave. *Guru* teaches us about *Waheguru*, who watches over us.

Anand is like a big reward from *Waheguru*, filling our hearts with joy and happiness. And *Anand Karaj*? Well, it is like a special party where two people get married, with Waheguru's blessings.

So, *Guru* teaches us about *Waheguru's* love, which fills us with *Anand*. And during *Anand Karaj*, we celebrate this love and happiness with everyone around us.

See how they are all connected? It is like a big circle of love and joy, with *Guru* and *Waheguru* at the centre, guiding us every step of the way.

And guess what? The best part is, we get to feast like kings and queens afterwards!

Isn't that amazing? Keep spreading love and happiness wherever you go!

ਸਤਿ ਸ੍ਰੀ ਅਕਾਲ:

ਵਾਹਿਗੁਰੂ ਜੀ ਕਾ ਖਾਲਸਾ ॥ ਵਾਹਿਗੁਰੂ ਜੀ ਕੀ ਫ਼ਤਹ

Sat Siri Akal & Waheguru Ji Ka Khalsa Waheguru ji Ki Fateh (KT)

Did you know that when we say, *"Sat Siri Akal"* and *"Waheguru Ji Ka Khalsa, Waheguru Ji Ki Fateh,"* we are tapping into something powerful?

Sat Siri Akal reminds us that truth is eternal and ever-present, guiding us to live with honesty and integrity in all that we do.

Waheguru Ji Ka Khalsa, Waheguru Ji Ki Fateh celebrates the triumph of morality and the noble spirit of the Khalsa community, inspiring us to uphold justice, equality, and compassion in our lives.

Together, they remind us of the power of truth and the victory of righteousness, guiding us on a path of courage, humility, and service.

Let us connect some more dots!

First, there's *Naam*, which is like a secret code that helps us feel close to Waheguru, our loving creator. It gives us a special connection with the universe, filling our hearts with love and peace.

Then, there's *Shabad*, which are beautiful verses from our Guru Granth Sahib Ji. These verses are messages from Waheguru, guiding us on how to live a good and happy life.

And when we say *Waheguru*, we are calling out to our best friend who is always there for us, ready to listen and help us through anything.

Chardikala is another amazing word. It is keeping our spirits high, like the sun shining bright no matter what and being brave, positive, and spreading joy wherever we go.

Sarbat da Bhalla is about wishing well for everyone. It says, "I hope everyone is happy and healthy." It is being kind, fair, and caring to everyone, just like our Guru teaches us.

Sat Siri Akal is a reminder that Waheguru is always with us, guiding us through every moment of our lives.

And when we say *Waheguru Ji Ka Khalsa, Waheguru Ji Ki Fateh*, we are declaring that we belong to Waheguru's army, where love and goodness always win.

Finally, there's *Anand*, which means true bliss and joy. Feeling happy and peaceful inside, knowing that Waheguru's love surrounds us.

So, remember these special words and let them fill your heart with love, courage, and kindness.

Keep shining bright!

ਉਦਮ ਦੀ ਕਹਾਣੀ

Udham's Short Story (KT)

And here is another story that captures what we have been learning. I hope you will enjoy this one too!

Once upon a time, in a vibrant village surrounded by tall, swaying trees and golden fields, there lived a spirited Sikh boy named Udham. Udham's eyes sparkled with curiosity, and his laughter echoed through the village like a melody of joy.

One bright morning, as Udham played near the glistening river, he stumbled upon a group of elders gathered beneath the shade of a majestic tree. Intrigued, he approached them, his heart fluttering with anticipation.

The elders welcomed him with warm smiles and invited him to join them. "We have a special story to share with you, dear Udham," one of them said gently. "It is a tale of Ek Onkar, the sacred symbol that reminds us of the divine oneness in all creation."

Eagerly, Udham listened as the elder spoke of Ek Onkar, the belief that there is one supreme creator who resides in everything and everyone. He learned that by recognizing this divine connection, one could understand their true essence, their Mool, and find peace and harmony within.

Inspired by the teachings of Ek Onkar, Udham embarked on a remarkable journey of self-discovery. Along the way, he encountered challenges and hurdles, but he faced them with unwavering courage, knowing that each trial was a part of his Karma, the actions that shape our destiny.

As Udham traversed the winding paths of life, he encountered the illusion of Maan and Maya, the temptation of worldly desires and ego. Through the guidance of wise mentors and the wisdom of his faith, he learned to embrace humility and to cherish the true treasures of the heart.

Guided by the divine grace of Gurprashad, Udham found solace in times of darkness and strength in moments of doubt. He understood that every twist and turn of his journey was guided by Waheguru Ji's will, and he surrendered herself to the path with unwavering trust.

With every step she took, Udham recited the sacred words of the Mool Mantar, Naam and Sarbat Da Bhalla, a prayer for the well-being of all humanity. He embraced the timeless truth of Sat Siri Akal and greeted each new day with the joyful cry of Waheguru Ji Ka Khalsa and Waheguru Ji Ki Fateh.

And so, dear friends, Udham's story continues to unfold, a testament to the power of faith, courage, and love. May his journey inspire us all to walk the path of righteousness and to spread kindness and compassion wherever we go.

Waheguru Ji Ka Khalsa! Waheguru Ji Ki Fateh!

ਗਿਆਨ

Key Teachings (KM)

The Guru Granth Sahib Ji teaches us some important things that can help us live better every day. Here are some of those special teachings:

Oneness of God: Always remember that there is one big, loving God who cares for everyone. So, be kind and loving to others, just like God loves us.

Equality for All: Everyone is important and equal, no matter where they come from or what they look like. Treat everyone with respect and fairness, whether they are your friends, family, or people you meet.

Importance of Truth: Always tell the truth. Being honest is super powerful and helps you build trust with others.

Sharing and Caring: Share what you have with others. Whether it is toys, snacks, or just being kind, sharing makes everyone happy.

Hard Work and Honest Living: Work hard and be honest in everything you do. Doing your best and being responsible makes you feel strong and proud.

Respect for Nature: Nature is a gift from God. Take care of the environment, plants, and animals. Be grateful for the beauty around you.

Contentment and Gratitude: Be thankful for what you have. Being grateful brings happiness. It is not always about having more; It is about appreciating what you have.

Helping Others: Help those who need it. Whether it is a friend who is sad or someone who needs assistance, offering help makes the world better.

Controlling Anger and Being Patient: When you feel angry, take a deep breath, and try to be patient. It is okay to feel emotions, but finding peaceful solutions is important.

Forgiveness: If someone makes a mistake, forgive them. Holding onto anger does not help. Forgiveness is like giving a gift to yourself.

Living in Harmony: Live peacefully with others. Embrace differences and learn from people who are different from you. It makes life more colourful and interesting.

Prayer and Meditation: Spend a moment each day for prayer or quiet time. It helps you connect with God and find peace within yourself.

Remember, these teachings are like a roadmap for a happy life. By following them, you can make the world a better place and be a shining light for others.

ਗੁਰਮਤ

Gurmat (KM)

We are at the end of our journey! As you embark on your journey into Sikhi, remember that you are on a path filled with love, wisdom, and adventure. Just like a brave explorer, you are discovering the beauty of your faith and all the wonderful teachings it holds.

Each step you take is like a new chapter in your amazing story, where you will learn about kindness, equality, and the power of Waheguru's love. Along the way, you will meet incredible people who will guide and inspire you, just like the Sikh Gurus and wise souls who came before us.

There may be challenges and obstacles on your journey, but do not worry! With the strength of your faith and the support of your Sangat, you will overcome anything that comes your way.

So, keep your heart open, your spirit strong, and your mind curious. Embrace each moment with joy and gratitude, knowing that you are on a path that leads to Waheguru's loving embrace.

Here are a few points to guide you along the way. This is called *Gurmat*, which just means "Guru's wisdom." Let us look at some of these special messages:

Believe in Yourself: Sikhi says that each person is unique and has a special light inside them from God. Believe in yourself, be confident, and know that you have special talents to share with the world.

Stay Humble and Kind: Even when you are confident, always stay humble. Treat everyone with kindness and respect, just like Guru Nanak taught about being humble and treating everyone equally.

Learn and Grow: Sikhs love learning. Be curious, ask questions, and never stop exploring innovative ideas. Learning helps you become the best version of yourself.

Be Honest and True: Guru Nanak said honesty is super important. Be honest with yourself and others. It is like having a solid foundation that helps you stand tall.

Practice Compassion: Sikhi is all about being kind and understanding. Feel what others feel and do-little acts of kindness. It makes the world a better place.

Face Challenges with Courage: Life can be tough, but Sikhi says be brave. Face problems with courage because you are strong enough to beat them.

Practice Simran (Remembering God - Waheguru): Take time to think and pray. Remembering God helps you find peace inside and stay connected to your spirit.

Help Others (Seva): Helping others is important in Sikhi. Doing small acts of kindness, like helping a friend or family member, helps you grow as a person.

Stay Positive (chardikala): Sikhi likes a cheerful outlook. Focus on the good stuff, be thankful, and spread happiness to others. Share your ideas, work together, and celebrate success with everyone.

Value Hard Work: Sikhi says working hard and earning an honest living is important. Putting effort into your goals helps you feel proud and happy.

Forgive and Let Go: Sikhi says forgiveness is key. Learn to forgive others and yourself. Holding onto grudges does not help anyone.

You are a shining star on this beautiful journey of Sikhi, and I can't wait to see all the amazing things you'll discover along the way. Keep shining bright!

Waheguru ji ka Khalsa, Waheguru ji ki Fateh!

ਪ੍ਰਿਤਾ

Beautiful Guidance for Any Era (KM)

The Siri Guru Granth Sahib has important messages that are still super relevant today. Let us look at a few:

On Equality: The Guru Granth Sahib tells us that everyone is equal, no matter who they are or where they come from. This is important today as we try to treat everyone with respect and include everyone in our communities.

On Service and Selflessness: It reminds us to help others without expecting anything in return. This is extra important now when there are lots of people who need help and support.

On Compassion and Empathy: The Guru Granth Sahib teaches us to care for all living things. With all the problems in the world, being kind and understanding to others is really needed.

On Inner Peace and Contentment: In our busy lives, it is important to find peace inside ourselves. Meditation and spiritual practice can help us feel calm and happy.

On Social Justice: It tells us to stand up against unfairness and treat everyone fairly. In a world where some people are treated badly because of who they are, this message is important.

On Environmental Stewardship: The Guru Granth Sahib reminds us to take care of nature and protect our planet. With so many environmental problems today, this is crucial for our future.

On Oneness and Unity: It teaches us that we are all connected and should work together. In a world where people often fight, this message of unity is important.

Here are some general rules for living by the teachings of the Siri Guru Granth Sahib Ji:

Meditation (Naam Simran): Spend time connecting with the divine every day through meditation.

Selfless Service (Seva): Help others without expecting anything back.

Reciting God's Name (Naam Japna): Think about and say God's name regularly for spiritual growth.

Honest Living (Kirat Karni): Work hard and be honest in everything you do.

Sharing (Vand Chakna): Share what you have, especially with those who need it.

Equality and Social Justice: Treat everyone fairly and stand up against unfairness.

Humility: Stay humble and recognize the goodness in everyone.

Respect for All Religions: Be respectful and open-minded towards people of all faiths.

Continuous Learning: Keep learning and improving yourself throughout your life.

Resilience and Endurance: Stay strong and keep going even when things get tough.

By following these teachings, we can make the world a better place and live happy, meaningful lives.

ਜੁਗਾਥੀ

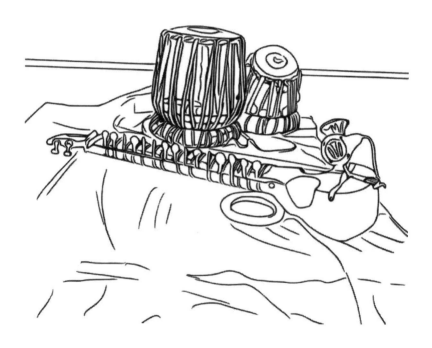

Practical tips for parents (KM)

Spreading Sikhi through everyday living involves incorporating the teachings and values of Sikhi into daily life in a simple and relatable manner. Here are practical ways to do so:

Storytelling: Share stories from Sikh history and scriptures that highlight values such as kindness, equality, and honesty. Make these stories engaging and relatable for children to understand.

Practicing Simran (Remembering God): Introduce short moments of reflection or prayer into daily routines. Encourage children to take a moment to be thankful, express gratitude, or think about the positive aspects of their day.

Promoting Seva (Selfless Service): Involve children in simple acts of kindness and service at home, in the community, or at local Sikh gurdwaras. It could be helping with chores, sharing toys, or participating in community events.

Celebrating Sikh Festivals: Celebrate Sikh festivals, such as Vaisakhi or Bandi Chor, with enthusiasm. Explain the significance of these celebrations and involve children in traditional rituals and festivities.

Incorporating Gurmukhi Learning: Introduce basic Gurmukhi letters and words to children. Learning the script can be a fun activity, and it lays the foundation for understanding Sikh scriptures in their original form.

Encouraging Equality and Respect: Emphasize the importance of treating everyone with respect and equality. Discuss the Sikh principles of oneness and how everyone, regardless of their background, is equal in the eyes of God.

Engaging in Family Discussions: Have open discussions about Sikh values and teachings during family meals or gatherings. Encourage children to express their thoughts and ask questions about Sikhi.

Living a Sustainable Lifestyle: Sikhi emphasizes respect for nature. Instruct children about environmental stewardship and sustainable living practices, connecting it to Sikh values of responsibility and care for the world.

Modelling Sikh Values: Be a positive role model by embodying Sikh values in your own actions. Children learn a lot through observation, so demonstrating kindness, honesty, and humility reinforces these values.

Creative Arts and Crafts: Engage children in creative activities that reflect Sikh teachings. This could include making art projects that depict stories from Sikh history or creating crafts related to Sikh festivals.

Attending Gurdwara Services: Regularly attend gurdwara services as a family. Participate in prayers, kirtan, and langar, and discuss the lessons learned during these visits with the children.

Encouraging Questions and Curiosity: Foster a curious mindset by encouraging children to ask questions about Sikhi. Create an environment where they feel comfortable exploring and understanding their faith.

By integrating these practices into everyday life, children can experience Sikhi as a vibrant and relevant part of their identity, fostering a deep connection to the rich values and teachings of Sikhi.

ਸਮਪਾਥੀ ਵਿਚ

A Closing Message (KM)

Hello wonderful friends,

In life's beautiful melody, let us feel the incredible rhythm that connects us all. Just like streams merging into the vast ocean, let us allow our hearts to blend with the love that surrounds us.

Remember, deep within each of us resides a special spark of divinity, shining brightly with truth and kindness. Let us treasure this divine essence within us and recognize it in everyone we encounter.

Live with humility, for it nurtures our spiritual growth. Let us break down the barriers of pride and recognize that we are all part of one big family.

Do what is right, guided by honesty, fairness, and justice. Let us stand up for what's right and work diligently to assist others.

Serve selflessly, offering our help without expecting anything in return. Let us perform acts of kindness with love, making our world a happier place.

Even during tough times, remember that every challenge teaches us valuable lessons. Let us face difficulties courageously, trusting in the guidance of a higher power.

Love wholeheartedly, as love is the greatest gift we can share. Let us spread love and kindness wherever we go, creating a more peaceful and joyful world.

May the teachings of the Guru Granth Sahib Ji illuminate our path, inspiring us to live with wisdom, grace, and love.

Let us journey forward together, hand in hand, spreading love and kindness wherever we roam.

With love and blessings,

Waheguru Ji Ka Khalsa, Waheguru Ji Ki Fateh

The Illustrator

Gurveer Padhal is a London-born Sikh artist, musician, and photographer. His visual works primarily focuses on the Indian Diasporas. Using film photography and with a background in art conservation, engagement and preservation of heritage is of upmost importance in his practice (gurveerpadhal@gmail.com)

ISBN 978-1-916838-88-8